# An Anthology of Ancient Egyptian Texts

# An Anthology of Ancient Egyptian Texts

## Life Through Literature

*Edited by*

CONSTANZE HOLLER

*Translated by*
Cordula Werschkun

First published in Great Britain in 2014 by
PEN & SWORD ARCHAEOLOGY
*an imprint of*
Pen and Sword Books Ltd
47 Church Street
Barnsley
South Yorkshire S70 2AS

Printed and bound in England
by CPI Group (UK) Ltd, Croydon, CR0 4YY

Typeset in Times New Roman by
CHIC GRAPHICS

*Pen & Sword Books Ltd incorporates the imprints of*
Pen & Sword Archaeology, Atlas, Aviation, Battleground, Discovery,
Family History, History, Maritime, Military, Naval, Politics, Railways,
Select, Social History, Transport, True Crime, Claymore Press,
Frontline Books, Leo Cooper, Praetorian Press, Remember When,
Seaforth Publishing and Wharncliffe.

*For* ~~a complete list of Pen & Sword titles please contact~~

47 Chu~~rch Street, Barnsley, South Yorkshire S70 2AS,~~ England
~~E-mail: enquiries@pen-and-sword.co.uk~~
~~Website: www.pen-and-sword.co.uk~~

# Contents

# Preface

Egyptian hieroglyphs fascinate us, but the stories they tell remain hidden from most of their observers. Therefore, in this volume texts have been compiled that will give an impression of the variety of the contents and genres of this literature from the Old to the New Kingdom, and a glimpse of Coptic. This is a book for anyone who is interested in ancient Egyptian literature and is looking for elegantly written, reliable translations intelligible to all beyond the academic editions.

*The biographical inscription of the soldier Amenemheb called Mehu* describes for the most part events that probably took place during the Syrian campaign of Tuthmosis III.

*The autobiography of Sinuhe* is doubtless the best known ancient Egyptian text and has even been adapted in literature and film.

The famous description of the attempt on the life of Amenemhat I is found in *The instructions of King Amenemhat I for his son Senwosret I*. Scholars still do not agree whether the pharaoh died during this event or survived.

In *The story of the shipwrecked sailor,* the sole survivor of a maritime disaster finds himself suddenly on an island ruled by a serpent deity.

The *Semna stele from the sixteenth year of the reign of King Senwosret III* marked the border of the Egyptian empire in the south and contains the general outline of the pharaoh's policy towards Nubia.

In *The tale of two brothers* – among other things – an unfaithful wife attempts to seduce her brother-in-law. This episode has a strong resemblance to the story about Potiphar's wife and Joseph.

Whether the representations of love, sexuality and partnership in *Ancient Egyptian love poems* can be regarded as actual historical fact is debatable. Yet they are without question a pleasure for the modern reader.

*The battle near Megiddo* took place at the beginning of the sole rule of Tuthmosis III. Numerous further campaigns of this pharaoh to the Near East followed, through which the Egyptian hegemony in the Eastern Mediterranean region during this period was underpinned.

*The tale of the prince and his three fates* is the life story of a prince foretold an unnatural death.

*Coptic Magic Spells* are incantations for love, healing and defence, curses and ritual collections with detailed instructions on what to do in which situations.

The selected texts are thus manifold and invite us on a journey to the beginnings of our own literature.

Constanze Holler
Mainz, August 2012

# The Biographical Inscription of the Soldier Amenemheb Called Mehu

*Andreas Hutterer*

The soldier Amenemheb, justified, speaks:

I was a very truthful servant of the ruler – life, prosperity, health – of devout heart for the king of Upper Egypt, and of useful mind to the king of Lower Egypt. I followed my lord on his campaigns through the northern and the southern foreign land, because he wanted me to be the companion of his two legs. When he was on the battlefields of his victories, his vigour strengthened my heart. I plundered in the foreign land of Negeba, and I took Asiatics – three men – prisoner. When His Majesty came to Naharina, I brought these three men there as booty, and I presented them to His Majesty as prisoners. The pillage on this campaign was repeated in the foreign land called the "juniper height" west of Kharbu. I took Asiatics prisoner, thirteen men, seventy live donkeys, thirteen bronze axes and gilded bronze. Repeated was the plunder on this campaign in the foreign country of Karkemish. I took prisoner. I crossed the "water of Naharina", while they were in my hand and I presented them to my lord. Consequently he rewarded me with a magnificent gift, namely in detail:

I saw the victories of the king of Upper and Lower Egypt, Men-kheper-Re – life be given to him – in the foreign land Sendjar, and he turned them (its inhabitants) into a great pile of corpses. After I had plundered before the eyes of the king and brought back a hand from there, the king gave me "gold of praise", namely in detail two silver rings.

And repeatedly I saw his bravery, when I was in his train. He conquered the city of Kadesh, while I did not leave his side. I took two people of the Maryannu prisoner, and I delivered them to the king, the lord of the two lands Tuthmosis, ruler of Thebes – may he live forever – and he gave me gold because of my valour before the eyes of all namely in detail from gold of the highest quality: a lion order, two *shebi* necklaces, two fly orders, four rings.

I saw my lord in all his manifestations in the foreign land of Pekhuu-netj it is called. I was the one who ascended to the head of the entire army.

Again I saw his victories in the foreign land of the wretched Tikhesi, in the place Meriu I plundered that place before the eyes of the king and took three Asiatics prisoner. As a consequence, my lord gave me "gold of praise", namely from gold: two *shebi* necklaces, two fly orders, a lion order, and, further, a female and a male servant.

And again I saw a further example of excellence that the lord of the two lands accomplished in Nyi. He hunted 120 elephants for their tusks. I seized the largest elephant among them as he attacked His Majesty. I was the one who cut off its tail when it was still alive, while I stood in the water between two stones. As a result my lord rewarded me with gold five garments.

Then the prince of Kadesh let loose a mare that was fast on her legs. She was in the process of penetrating the lines of the Egyptian troops when I chased after her on my two legs, armed with my dagger. And I opened her body, cut off her tail and presented it to the king. They [the troops] praised god for it. The king showed joy, and the same joy seized me. Pleasure took over my body.

Now His Majesty let all brave men in his army step forward in order to storm the new wall erected by the people of Kadesh. I was the one who stormed it at the head of all brave men. No one else had achieved such a thing before me. The result was that I took two men of the Maryannu people prisoner. And my lord rewarded me once more because of this with all magnificent things of joy of heart.

I accomplished all this plunder when I was a soldier of the battleship called Amun-user-hat. I was the one who made ropes on Amun-user-hat, and I was at the head of its team during rowing for Amun during the beautiful festival of Ipet, when the two lands were in elation.

Then the king of Upper and Lower Egypt had completed his lifespan of numerous perfect years in valour, in might, and justified, from year one to year fifty-four of his reign, month three of the *peret* season, last day, under the majesty of the king of Upper and Lower Egypt, Men-kheper-Re, justified. He departed to the sky, was united with the solar disc, and the divine body was united with the one who had created him. Yet when the land became light again, in the morning when Aten appeared shining and the sky was clear, the king of Upper and Lower Egypt was Aa-kheperu-Re, son of Re Amenhotep, god and ruler of Thebes – life may be given to him – placed on the throne of his father. He rested in the palace and consolidated his rule. After he had campaigned against the people of Qat he beheaded their princes, appearing as Horus, son of Isis. He seized the Wentiu people and the Kenemtiu people, and every country bowed before his power, their tributes on their backs, so that the breath of life was given to them.

Then His Majesty saw me rowing under him in his falcon ship – "Amenhotep, god and ruler of Thebes-has-appeared-in-the-barque" was its name – when I was rowing during the beautiful festival of Ipet and also to Djeser-akhet. When I had gone ashore, I was brought to the audience hall of the palace, and I was made to step in front of the son of Amun, Aa-kheperu-Re, great in strength. There I lay prostrate before His Majesty, and he said to me: "I got to know your character when I was still a child and you were still in the retinue of my father. I wish to appoint you to an important office: you shall lead the army for me according to my command. And you shall be in charge of the king's guard." Then the commander Mehu carried out what his lord said.

# The Autobiography of Sinuhe

*Agnes Klische*

The local prince and nome governor, seal-bearer of the king of Upper and Lower Egypt, sole companion, judge and head of the nomes of the ruler – life, prosperity, health – in the lands of the Asiatics, the true royal acquaintance beloved by him, the retainer/courtier Sinuhe, he says: "I was a retainer obedient to his lord, servant in the royal harem of the hereditary princess, the highly praised, wife of King Senwosret I in Khenem-sut, daughter of King Amenemhat I in Ka-Nefer, Neferu, the venerable mistress."

It is the thirtieth year of the reign, month three of the inundation season, day seven: entrance of the god into his horizon. The king of Upper and Lower Egypt, Sehetep-ib-Re ascended to the sky and is united with the sun disc. The divine body is joined with the one who has created it. The residence was in deep silence, the hearts were full of mourning, the great double gate was closed. The court had their heads on their knee while the people were lamenting. Yet His Majesty had sent an army to the land of the Libyans at the head of which his eldest son, the perfect god Senwosret, I stood as commander. He had been sent in particular to beat the foreign lands and to punish the inhabitants of Libya. Meanwhile he was on the way back and brought prisoners as well as innumerable herds from Libya.

Therefore, the courtiers of the palace sent news to the western bank of the Nile in order to inform the royal son about the situation in the palace. The messengers met him in the early evening on the road. Not an instant he hesitated, the falcon rose with his retinue, but without informing the soldiers. At the same time the other royal children had been informed, who were behind him among the troops. It was called out to one of them, while I was standing there by chance and heard the voice. When he made his report, I was found undetected in the immediate vicinity of the conspiracy. My heart became confused, my arms spread wide, and I began to tremble in every limb. Then I slunk off at a hurried pace, in order to find a 'silent spot'. I hid among the bushes to clear the path for the one walking on it.

Thereupon I set out on a journey south, but did not intend to reach the residence, for I assumed that an uprising was brewing, which I did not hope to survive. I travelled to Maati, to the area of sanctuary of the sycamore, landed on the island of Snofru and spent a day on the margins of the fertile land. At daybreak I set out and encountered a man standing by the side of my road – and he greeted me, who was afraid of him. When the day turned into evening I reached the village of the cattle. I crossed on a barge without rudder, only aided by a wisp of the western wind. I passed the eastern side of Iku, above the sanctuary of the Lady of the Red Mountain. After I had marched northwards on the road, I reached the Walls of the Ruler, which had been erected for the defence against the Asiatics and the subjugation of the Bedouins. I took cover in a shrub because I feared to be seen by the guards on the fortress wall. Only at night time I continued my journey and arrived at Peten, after the land had got light. I settled on an island in the Bitter Lakes. A bout of thirst seized me, I was dehydrated and my throat as dry as dust. I thought to myself: This is the (fore)taste of death. Then, however, I drew new courage and got up, because I heard the bellow of cattle and spotted some Bedouins. Their sheikh recognised me, because he had been to Egypt. THe gave me water, milk was brought to me, and I went with him to his tribe. How wonderful it was what they did for me.

From then on, one foreign land passed me on to the next. I broke away from Byblos and went to Kedem. There I spent half a year, when Amunenshi – the ruler of Upper Retjenu – called me and said to me: 'You will prosper with me. You will hear the language of Egypt.' He said this because he knew my character and had heard of my practice. The people of Egypt who were there with him had championed my case and spoke of me. He wanted to know from me: 'For which reason did you come here? Did something happen in the residence?'

I answered him: 'The king of Upper and Lower Egypt, Sehetep-ib-

Re, has gone to the horizon. I do not know what happened afterwards.' The following I relayed only as half-truth: 'When I was returning with an army from the land of the Libyans, it was reported to me. My *ib* heart became weak, my *hati* heart was no longer inside my body – and got me on to the roads of flight. Nothing has been charged against me, nobody spit into my face. No bad utterance was heard about me and my name was not proclaimed by heralds. I have no idea who or what has brought me to this foreign land. It was like the plan of a god, as if a man from the Delta finds himself on Elephantine or a man of the marshes in Nubia.'

Amunenshi asked me: 'How does that land exist without him, the excellent god, the fear of whom has passed through the foreign lands like Sekhmet in a year of plague?'

This was my answer to him: 'Indeed, his son has entered the palace and has taken up the legacy of his father. He, too, is a god. He is second to none. No one else has come before him. He is master of wisdom, brilliant in plans and superior in messages, according to his order they set out and return. He was the one crossing the foreign countries, while his father was in the residence, and he notified him that this which he had ordered had been executed. He has a strong personality, takes action himself, and is valiant. There is nobody equal to him, when he falls upon the Nine Bow peoples and approaches the thick of the battle. He is one who lowers the horn like a bull in attack, one who paralyses hands. His enemies cannot hold the battle lines. He is one who stains his face when skulls are cleft. One cannot withstand in his proximity. He runs in great strides, when he devastates the fleeing. Nobody who turns his back on him comes to a conclusion. His heart is steadfast in the moment of storm. He is one who turns around, never does he think of retreat. He is brave even when he sees the numerically superior multitude. He does not permit lethargy in his heart. He is courageous when he sees the horde. It is his joy to apply himself to the thick of the fight. When he seizes his shield, he is already amidst the battle. He does not have to raise his arm twice in order to kill. There is nobody who could evade his weapon, nobody who could draw his bow. The Nine Bow peoples flee before his arms like before the might of the great uraeus snake. Before he commences to fight, he has already planned the end. He allows himself neither rest nor tranquillity.

'He is the lord of mercy, great in popularity, he conquers with love. His town loves him more than itself, it rejoices more about him than its town god; men and women pass by in exultation about him, for he is king. Already before birth he seized possession of everything; his face is turned towards this since his birth. He made wealthy those who were born with him. He is the only one given by god. This land is in joy that it is now ruled by him. He expands the borders and will take possession of the southern lands; he is not yet thinking of the northern lands. He was created to beat the Asiatics and to subjugate the Bedouins. Send message to him. Take care that he knows your name. Do not utter any curse against His Majesty. He will do good without fail for the country that is obedient to him on its water.'

Amunenshi answered me, being amused: 'Well, then Egypt prospers, since it knows that he is strong. Look, you however are here and will remain with me. Good will be that which I will make for you.'

He placed me at the head of his children and married me to his eldest daughter. He gave me the opportunity to choose for myself a plot of his land, from the choice part of this which was his property to the borders of the next foreign land. It was a beautiful country, Yaa was its name, and there was nothing of equal value to it. Therein were fig trees together with vines, it possessed more wine than water. Great amounts of honey were there, numerous olive trees, all kind of fruits grew on its trees. Barley was there and wheat, unlimited was the number of all cattle. Of great extent was also this which was added due to my popularity.

Amunenshi appointed me as ruler of a tribe, one of the choicest tribes of his country. Every day fresh food was prepared for me, and wine was delivered daily, cooked meat and grilled poultry, besides desert game. Traps were set on my behalf, and they hunted for me, in addition to the prey brought by my dogs. They produced innumerable sweets for me, and there was milk in every form. So I spent many years while my children grew into strong people each man became one who had conquered his tribe.

The messenger travelling north or south to the residence used to stop off with me. I let all people stay with me, I gave water to the thirsty. I set right the one who had lost his way, I saved the one who had been robbed. I counselled the rulers of the foreign lands in their defence against the Asiatics, for they prepared to offer fierce resistance. This ruler of Retjenu (Amunenshsi) enabled me to have numerous years as leader of his army. Each foreign land against which I campaigned was beaten by me, so that it was driven off from its fodder plants and its wells. I captured its herds, seized its inhabitants and pillaged their food. That I killed the people in it was by my strength, with my bow, through my strategy and my excellent plans. I was useful to his (Amunenshi's) heart and he loved me, because he had seen my courage. He placed me at the head of his children because he saw that my arms were mighty.

One day a strong man came from Retjenu and challenged me in my own tent. He was a brave man without his equal, he had conquered the land of Retjenu to its borders. He said he wanted to fight against me and intended to kill me and capture my herds, all according to the counsel of his tribe. Because of this the ruler Amunenshi conferred with me. I said to him: 'Indeed, I do not know him and I am not his ally, so that I might have walked about his camp unhindered. Or is it the case that I had opened the back of his house and climbed over his fences? It is the pure malice of his heart, because he sees me carrying out your commissions. I am actually like a peaceful bull of the *huu* cattle amongst another herd, when the bull of a wild herd attacks him and the long horn cattle seizes him. Is a humble man as beloved as a chief? No Nine Bow man consorts with a Lower Egyptian. What is the point to plant a papyrus stem in the mountains? Is there a breeding bull that loves to fight, or a fighting bull that will turn away in fright of the one wishing to lock horns with it? If it is his wish to fight, so he may utter this wish. Is there a god who does not know what he has pre-ordained, he who knows how everything is arranged?'

During the night I prepared myself. I drew my bow, cleaned and arranged my weapons, laid out my dagger. The day had hardly dawned when Retjenu came and gathered his tribes. He had called together the foreign lands allied with him and planned this fight. Then he came to me, while I rose and went near him, observant and braced for all eventualities.

Every *hati* heart burnt for me, the wives chattered anxiously, every *ib* heart felt pity for me. They said: 'Is there no other strong man who could fight against him?'

Thereupon his shield, his battle axe and his armful of spears fell before me. I let his weapons thus approach me and pass me by. His arrows went astray, one after the other. Then he made a dash for me, because he intended to beat me. When he had approached near enough, I shot at him and my arrow struck his neck. Then he cried out, fell onto his nose, and I killed him with his own battle axe. I emitted my war cry when I stood over him, while every Asiatic was in lament. I gave praise to Monthu while his subjects mourned for him.

Because of this the ruler Amunenshi embraced me. Subsequently I fetched the possessions of the strong man and robbed his herd. That which he had intended to do to me I now did to him. I took away that which was in his tent and plundered his camp. Because of this I became powerful, rich in possessions and countless cattle. So a god has acted in order to be favourable to one against whom he had been wroth and whom he had banished to another country. Today his (the god's) heart is pacified. A runaway flew because of his ambiguous situation, now my good reputation is in the residence. A creeping man crawled because of hunger, now I give bread to my neighbour. A man left his country due to poverty, now I own white royal linen and the best linen cloth. A man runs errands himself due to the lack of somebody he might send, now I am rich in people.

My house is beautiful, my place spacious, but my thoughts are in the palace. Oh every god who has pre-ordained this flight, may you be merciful and may you return me to the residence. You have determined for me that which is unknown, may you now be lenient towards me as someone justified. Hopefully you will let it happen that I will see the place again in which my heart still resides. Is there anything greater than that my corpse is reunited with the land in which I was born? Your call 'Come behind me' is actually the cause of this happy event. May the god give me contentment. May he act accordingly so to shape a better end for the one whom he has caused grief. May his heart have pity with he who he has banished to live in a foreign country. Is he not today the one who is merciful? So he may hear the supplicant from afar, may he reach out his arm to he who has roamed the land because of him to the place to which he had brought him.

May the king of Egypt, too, be in charity with me so that I may live in his mercy, greet the mistress of the land who is in his palace and listen to the commissions of their children. Alas, may my limbs be rejuvenated, for age has come to me and weakness has caught up with me. My eyes are heavy, my arms slack and my legs have ceased to follow the tired heart. I have approached my demise. They shall lead me to the places of the *neheh* eternity. May I follow the mistress of the universe. Alas, may they speak well of me to their children, may they spend the *neheh* eternity above me.

And indeed His Majesty, king of Upper and Lower Egypt, Kheper-ka-Re, justified, had been informed about this my situation. Therefore His Majesty sent me gifts, as they are only given by the king, and he pleased the heart of my humble self equal to the ruler of any foreign land. The royal children who were in his palace sent me their message.

*Copy of the order that was brought to the servant regarding his return to Egypt:*

Horus name: living since birth; two-Ladies name: living since birth; king of Upper and Lower Egypt: Kheper-ka-Re; son of Re: Senwosret I, he may live from the *djet* eternity to the *neheh* eternity. Order of the king to the retainer/courtier Sinuhe: behold, this order of the king is brought to you to let you know the following: you have roamed the foreign lands, have gone from Kedem to Retjenu, Foreign land passed you to foreign land solely because of the counsel of your heart. What have you actually done that one should have acted against you? You did not curse so that one might have rejected your words. Your name was not mentioned in the various discourses so that you might have feared rejection. You did not speak unasked in the council of the wise so that one might have opposed your utterances. This plan that your heart had made for you, it did not really exist in my heart against you.

This your queen lives in the palace, perpetually and consistently, on her head is the rule of the land and her children are in the privy council. You shall amass the splendours that they give to you, and you will live off their gifts. Oh, come back to Egypt. You shall see the residence where you grew up; you shall kiss the ground before the great double gate and join the 'friends' of the court. It is the way that you have commenced age and your virility lessens. Oh, think of the day of burial, the guidance to the state of veneration [the spirit state]. The night watch is carried out for you with anointment and bandages from the hands of the goddess Tait. The funeral procession is arranged for you on the day of interment, and the inner coffin is made out of gold, the head piece from lapis lazuli. The sky is above you, after you have been placed into a casket. Cattle will pull the sledge with your coffin, musicians will be at the head of your procession, and the 'dance of the tired' is performed at the entrance to your tomb. The requirement in food for the offering is recited for you, and they slaughter for you at the entrance to your offering place. The pillars of your tomb are from white stone, constructed in the midst of the tombs of the royal children. Your death will not take place in this foreign country and you will not be buried by Asiatics. Neither will you be wrapped into a ram's fleece, nor a simple tomb will be erected for you. This flight already endures longer than it needs time to roam the land! May you think of your corpse and return!

This order reached me and was read to me when I was surrounded by my tribe. Thereupon I threw myself into the dust onto my belly and I sprinkled it onto my body. I circled my camp in elation with the words: 'How shall this be understood and judged in reference to a servant whose heart has led him to far-away lands? Oh, how good is the forbearance that saves from the hand of death. You *ka* will cause that I will be in the residence when I die.'

*Copy of the answer to this order:*

The servant of the palace, Sinuhe, says: 'In very beautiful peace! Concerning: this flight which my humble self has undertaken in his ignorance. It is your *ka*, perfect god, lord of the two lands, beloved of Re, praised by Monthu, lord of Thebes, Amun, lord of the thrones of the two lands, Sobek-Re, Horus, Hathor, Atum wih his ennead, Sopdu, Neferbau-Semseru, the eastern Horus

20

and the lady of Imhet – she may attend your head – the council of gods that rules over the inundation, Horus-Min who is guest in the foreign lands, Wereret, lady of Punt, Nut and Haroëris-Re, as well as all gods of Egypt and of the islands in the sea: they may give life and lordship onto your nose, they shall provide you with their gifts and may give to you the *neheh* eternity without boundaries, the *djet* eternity without limit. May the fear of you remain established in the foreign lands and in the mountain territories, may this be conquered for you which is encompassed by the sun. This is the entreaty of a humble servant to his lord who comes to the rescue from the west. Lord of knowledge who understands the subjects, may he recognise as king in the palace that the servant Sinuhe fears to express it, as it is like a matter too great to be repeated.

The great god, the image of Re, recognises even he who is low. The subject is in the hand of him who cares for him, he is truly subject to his plan. Your Majesty is Horus the conqueror, strong are both your arms against all lands. So Your Majesty may order that Meki from Kedem, Khentijaush from Khentkeshu and Menes from the Phoenician lands shall be fetched, because they are renowned, good rulers who have grown up in love to you – not to forget Retjenu which belongs to you just like its dogs.

This flight that my humble self undertook was not in my heart and my intention, and I did not know what separated me from this place in the residence. It was like a dream state, or as if a man from the Delta finds himself on Elephantine, or a man of the marshes in Nubia. I was not feared, nobody pursued me, no one talked badly about me, and my name was not heard from the mouth of the herald. There was only this trembling of my limbs, when my feet hurried away, my heart seduced me and the god who had preordained this flight began to pull me away. After all, I had not been arrogant previously, since a man knowing his country is in awe, because Re has spread the fear of you everywhere in the land and the terror of you in every foreign country.

Whether I am in the residence or at this place here, you are the one who darkens this horizon. The sun rises because of love to you, and the water in the rivers is drunk when you wish it. The air of the sky is breathed when you say it. My humble self will bequeath the office of vizier, which I held in this place here. May Your Majesty act as you like. One lives of the air that you give. May Re, Horus and Hathor love this your noble nose, of which Monthu, the lord of Thebes, desires that it may live forever.

On route to the residence I was permitted to halt in Yaa, so that I could bequeath my possessions to my children. My eldest son was the keystone of my tribe and with him all my property was in good hands: my subjects, my entire cattle, my fruits and all the sweet fruit trees. So I finally set off and travelled southwards, whereby I stopped on the Ways of Horus. I reached the commander of the frontier guard on the Walls of the Rulers, who sent message of my arrival to the residence. Thereupon His Majesty sent an excellent overseer of the royal agricultural workers. With him came ships laden with gifts, as they are only given by the king, namely for the Asiatics who journeyed with me as my companions on the Ways of Horus – I knew each of them by name.

After I had thus decamped and set sail, each overseer performed his task. They mashed and brewed at my side until I reached the place of the ruler. When the land became light, very early in the morning, someone came who called me, while ten men came and ten men went to lead me to the palace. With my head I touched the ground between the statues, while the royal children, who had stood in the niches, came toward me. The 'friends' of the court who commonly make the introductions to the audience hall, took me to the privy council. I found His Majesty on a large throne in a niche made of electrum. Suddenly I was lying on my stomach and did not know what happened to me in his presence, while this god spoke to me and greeted me in a friendly manner. Yet I was like a man seized by dimness. My *ba* soul had passed away, my limbs were weak, my *hati* heart was no longer inside my body. I could no longer distinguish between life and death. Therefore His Majesty remarked to one of these 'friends': 'Lift him up and let him speak to me!' And His Majesty continued: 'Well, well, you have returned. You have roamed the foreign lands, after you had fled. There you have encountered old age, after you had completed the years accordingly. The burial of your corpse will not be squalid, for you will not be interred by the Bow People. However, do not be silent again. You have not spoken, although your name was called because you fear punishment.'

Thereupon I gave answer as someone nevertheless still in fear: 'What is it that my lord says to me? If I answer, it is not by my free will, but through the hand of god. Terror is inside my body, such as the kind that caused the flight then pre-ordained. Behold, I am before you. My life belongs to you. Your Majesty may act as you like!'

Now the royal children were beckoned and His Majesty remarked to the royal wife: 'Look, Sinuhe has come as an Asiatic, as a creature of the Bedouins.'

Then she emitted a very loud cry in dismay, while the royal children were in one great clamour. Hereupon she asked His Majesty in disbelief: 'But this is not really him, oh ruler, my lord?'

His Majesty simply replied: 'Indeed, it is truly him.' They fetched their menits, clappers and sistrums and presented these to His Majesty with the words: 'Reach out for these beautiful instruments, gracious king, the jewel of the mistress of the sky. May the Golden One give life to your nose and may the mistress of the stars unite herself with you. Northwards travels the Upper Egyptian crown, southwards the Lower Egyptian one, united and completed by your utterance. The green uraeus is placed onto your forehead so that evil spells are warded off from you. Re, lord of the two lands, be merciful to you. They rejoice about you as about the mistress of the universe. Discard your spear. Lift your horn. Put down your arrows. Give air to him in trouble breathing. Give us your beautiful festival offering on this festive day. This is this sheikh, a son of the north wind, a Bow Man born in Egypt. He had fled in fear of you, he had left the country in terror of you. Yet there is no timidity in the face of the one who sees the face of the king. There is no fear in the eye looking upon you.'

Yet His Majesty reassured them: 'He does not need to fear and will not tremble in terror. He will be a friend among the high officials and admitted to the court. Just go now to the morning council to prepare him!'

So I left the interior of the council chamber, the royal children put out their hands to me, and we went out of the great double gate. I was brought to the house of a prince with many precious things: a bathroom and 'images of the horizon', jewellery from the treasury, clothes from royal linen, incense and the finest royal ointment as well as his favourite officials in each room. Each steward performed his duties and the traces of the years left my body. My beard was removed, my hair combed, the dirt was given to the desert and the clothes to the inhabitants of the sand. I was dressed in the finest linen cloth and salved with fine ointments. I spent the night in a bed, after I had given the sand to those living in it, and the simple oil of the tree to the one anointing himself with it.

The house of the 'lord of the pond' was donated to me, which had been in the hand of a 'friend'. Numerous craftsmen were in the process of renovating it, each tree was planted correctly. Food from the palace was brought to me three or four times a day, in addition to that which the royal children gave. Never were these deliveries interrupted. A tomb was constructed for me, a pyramid from stone, in the midst of the royal pyramids. The overseer of the pyramid craftsmen prepared the ground. The overseer of the treasury officials was recording. The overseer of the sculptors was carving. And the overseer of the workmen, who were at the tomb complexes, also busied himself with it. The entire equipment that is placed in a tomb was manufactured there. Mortuary priests were allocated to me, a garden complex with fields was laid out for me, which is located on the outskirts of the site of the tomb, as it is done for a select 'friend'. My statue was gilded, its kilt covered in electrum – His Majesty had ordered its manufacture. Never was there a lowly man for whom the equal was done. I was in the favour of the king – until the 'day of landing' came.

It has taken place from its beginning to its end as that which was found in writing.

# The Instructions of King Amenemhat I For His Son Senwosret I

*Meike Becker*

Beginning of the instructions that the King Sehetep-ib-Re, son of Re Amenemhat I, justified, has composed. He speaks to his son, the master of the universe, and explains the truth to him. After he has appeared as a god, he says: 'Listen to that which I will say to you, so that you will reign better over the land and rule the two river banks of Egypt more than well.

'Yet beware of the lowly servants, even if no thought was lost on their deceit so far. Do not approach them in your solitude. Do not trust any brother. Do not recognise any friend. Do not create confidantes. For this has no success. You shall sleep in the manner that your own heart guards you, since a man will not find any support on the day of misfortune.

'I have given to the poor, nurtured the orphan and let the have-not reach the goal just as the proprietor.

'The one having eaten my food made allegations against me.

'The one to whom I had put out my arms used this for schemes.

'Those dressed in my fine linen garments, they look upon me like a needy one dressed in grass.

'Those who had been salved with my myrrh pour water over it.

'My living images and the part of the people usually on my side have hatched a plot against me, as it has been unheard of so far, and a conflict the dimensions of which have not been seen yet.

'However, if one fights on the battleground and will forget the past, then there will be no success for the one who cannot assess his knowledge.

'It was after supper, when night fell, and after I had received an hour of heart's joy. I rested tired on my bed and my heart had begun to follow my slumber.

'Then suddenly the weapons meant for protection were wielded above me, while I behaved like a desert snake. After I was awoken by the fight, my limbs obeyed me once again. When I found out that it was a frenzied fight of the bodyguard, I hastily seized the weapons with my hand and caused the cowards to retreat due to a counter-attack – yet there is no brave man in the night and nobody who fights alone. Without a protector there is no guarantee for success.

'Behold, the assassination happened, when you were not there, before the court had heard that I wish to bequeath my office to you, and before I had conferred with you. Now I want to settle your matters. Because I had not thought about it and my heart had not suspected the untrustworthiness of the body of servants, I was not yet prepared for it.

'Have women ever mustered troops for battle in the past? Have troublemakers ever been raised inside the palace before? Yet does not the dam break, too, when the water softens the soil, so that the poor are deprived of the fruits of their labour?

'Since my birth no injustice has been done to me and nothing comparable to my misfortune has happened to a man performing brave deeds.

'I entered Elephantine and travelled to the marshes of the Delta. When I busied myself with the frontier of the land, I realised its innermost needs. Due to the strength of my arms and of my personality I reached the boundaries of Egypt.

'I am the one who created the grain, a favourite of Nepri, after Hapi had treated me respectfully at each spring. In the years of my reign nobody suffered hunger or thirst. They can live comfortably because of what I have done, and then talk about me. For everything I have ordered is in the right place.

'I have tamed lions and caught crocodiles, subjugated the settled inhabitants of Wawat and captured the nomadic population of Medja. Furthermore, I let the Asiatics follow me like a dog.

'I built for myself a blazing house of gold, the ceilings of which are of lapis lazuli. The walls are of silver, the floors of stone, the doors of copper and the bolts of bronze. It is made for eternity and prepared for infinity. I know this because I am the lord of everything.

'Now there is, however, much accusatory talk on the streets. The wise man agrees, the fool negates it in opposition, as he does not know it and is negligible in your view.

'Oh Senwosret, my son, both my legs pass away, while my own heart approaches you and both my eyes rest on you. The children are at the side of the sun people in an hour of heart's joy and they give praise to you.

'Behold, I have arranged the past so that I can order the future for you. I will conclude that which is in my heart for you. For you bear the white crown of the divine progeny. That means that the matters are at their places accordingly, as I have pre-arranged it for you.

'I had hardly boarded the barque of Re than the kingship had risen again, like at the beginning, just as that which I created of it within it.

'Erect your monuments. Complete your burial chamber.

'Take note of the wisdom of the man with a wise heart, because you wish him to be on the side of Your Majesty – life, prosperity, health.'

*Colophon*

This means that it comes to a good and satisfying end.

For the *ka* soul of the diligent lauded one, he of good character, the scribe of the treasury Qagabut (and for the *ka* soul) of the scribe of the treasury Hori.

# The Tale of the Shipwrecked Sailor

## *Anja Hilbig*

*A royal envoy is anxious after a seemingly unsuccessful expedition how he will face his king on arrival. One of his followers has heard his lamentations and wants to comfort him.*

The capable follower said: 'Be glad, oh prince! For behold, we have reached the residence, the mallet was seized and the mooring post driven into the ground, the rope at the bow now lies on land. Praise was given, god was praised, and everybody embraces his comrade. Our crew has returned safe and sound, our soldiers suffered no loss. We reached the boundaries of Wawat and passed the island of Biga. Behold, we have returned in peace, and we have reached our country.

'Listen to me, my prince. I do not exaggerate. Wash yourself and pour water over your fingers. Answer only if you have been addressed, and talk to the king with confident heart. Answer without stammering. For the words of a man can save him, and his speech can achieve leniency. Yet you will do anyway as you wish. It is tiring to encourage you.

'I want to tell you something similar that happened to me. I travelled to the mines of the ruler and crossed the sea in a ship with the length of 120 cubits and the width of 40 cubits. One-hundred-and-twenty sailors, among the best of Egypt, were on board. Whether they looked to the sky or whether they observed the sea – their hearts were more valiant than those of lions. Even before a storm sprung up, they predicted it, just like a tempest before it broke.

'Yet a storm had broken, when we were still at sea, before we had reached land. And the wind sprung up, blew harder and harder and whipped up a wave of 8 cubits. Only the mast was broken by the wave, but the ship sank nonetheless. Of those on board none remained. I, however, was carried by a wave of the sea to an island and spent three

29

days there alone. Only my heart was my companion. I slept under the cover of a tree and in its shadow. Then I rose to my feet to explore what edible things I might put into my mouth.

'I found figs and grapes there and all manner of delicious vegetables. There were ripe and green sycamore fruits, and cucumbers as if they had been planted. Fish and fowl were there too. There was nothing missing on this island. Then I ate my fill and put aside what my arms could not carry. Thereon I took the fire-making drill. I had hardly fanned a fire before I also made a burnt offering to the gods.

'Then I suddenly heard a thundering noise and thought it was a wave of the sea. Trees splintered and the earth quaked. When I took the hands from my eyes I saw it was a snake approaching. It measured 30 cubits and its beard was more than 2 cubits long. Its limbs were covered with gold and its eyebrows were of real lapis lazuli. It reared towards the front. It opened its mouth to me, while I lay before it on my belly, and it spoke to me: "Who has brought you here, who has brought you here, little one? If you do not tell me who has brought you to this island, I will take care that you will find yourself as ash – having turned into someone who had never been seen!

'You speak to me, but I cannot hear you. I lie before you and do not recognise myself."

'Then it grabbed me by its mouth and brought me to its resting place. There it lay me down without hurting me. I was sound, nothing was done to me. It opened its mouth, while I lay before it on my belly, and spoke to me: "Who has brought you here, who has brought you here, little one? Who has brought you to this island in the sea, the borders of which are entirely surrounded by water?"

'Then I answered. My arms were bent in awe, as I said to it: "It so happened that I travelled to the mines by order of the king, in a ship of 120 cubits length and 40 cubits width. One-hundred-and-twenty sailors of Egypt's choicest were on board. Whether they looked to the sky or to the sea – their hearts were more valiant than those of lions. Even before a storm sprung up, they predicted it just like a tempest before it broke. Each of them had a more courageous heart and a stronger arm than his companion. No fool was among them.

'"Yet a storm had sprung up, when we were still at sea, before we had reached land. And the wind rose, blew harder and harder and whipped up a wave of 8 cubits. Only the mast was broke by the wave, but the ship sank nonetheless. Of those on board none remained – but me. And look, now I am here with you. For I was carried to the island by a wave of the sea."

'Thereupon the snake said to me: "Do not be afraid, do not be afraid, little one. You do not need to turn pale because you are now with me. For behold, a god has let you live and brought you to the island of the *ka*. There is nothing missing on the island and it is full of all good things.

'Behold, you will spend month upon month on this island, until four months will have passed. Then a ship from your native land will come with sailors who you know. You will return to the residence with them and are allowed to die in your city. Alas, how happy is the one who can report his adventures when the misfortunes have already passed. I will now tell you something similar that happened on this island.

'I lived here with my siblings, and children were among us too. Together with my children and relatives we counted seventy-five snakes, and I will not even mention my little daughter, who was given to me as the answer to a prayer. Then suddenly a star fell down and all went up in flames because of it. This happened when I was not with them, they burnt to death, while I was not among them. And I nearly died when I found them as a single pile of corpses.

'Yet if you are brave and your heart strong, then you will be able to embrace your children once again. You will kiss your wife, you will see your house again, and that is more beautiful than everything else. You will reach your homeland and live there amidst your relatives."

'I remained stretched out on my belly and touched the ground before it: "I want to thank you: I will report your might to the king and make your greatness known to him. I will ensure that ladanum and ointment, incense and balm are brought to you as well as frankincense for the temples with which every god is satisfied. I will tell what has happened to me and what I have seen of your power. They will thank you in the city before the officials of the entire country. I will slaughter cattle for you as burnt offerings and will sacrifice fowl to you. I will let ships be brought to you laden with all manner of precious objects from Egypt. So as it is done for a god who loves the people, in a faraway land unknown to them."

'Then the snake laughed about me and about that which I had said. It seemed foolish to it and it said to me: "You have actually not much myrrh, you are only the owner of frankincense. I, however, am the ruler of Punt and the myrrh belongs to me. This ointment you are promising to me exists in abundance on the island. And when the time has come that you will leave this place, then you will never see this island again, because it will have foundered."

'One day this ship came, as the snake had predicted. I started to run, climbed a high tree and immediately recognised those who were on board. Thereupon I went to the snake in order to report this to it – but it already knew. And it said to me: "Keep well, keep well, little one, until home For you will see your children again. Spread my good reputation in your city. See, this is what I wish of you."

'Thereon I threw myself on the ground before the snake and bent my arms in awe before it. It gave me a cargo of myrrh and ointment, incense and balm, *tishep* wood, *shasekh* perfume and eye make-up, tails of giraffes, a large piece of frankincense, elephant tusks, greyhounds, long-tailed and short-tailed monkeys, baboons and all manners of riches. I loaded everything aboard and once again threw myself onto my belly in order to thank the snake.

'Then it said to me: "Behold, you will reach the residence in two months' time and you will embrace your children. You will feel young again at home, and later you will be buried there." I descended to the shore near the ship and greeted the crew on board. At the strand I gave praise to the lord of the island, and those on board did the same.

'We sailed northwards to the residence of the king. After two months we reached home, just as the snake had said. I received an audience with the ruler and presented him the gifts I had brought from the island. And he thanked me in front of the officials of the entire country, promoted me to a follower and provided me with 200 servants. Look at me, after I have reached my land and am looking back on my past adventures. Listen to my speech. For look, it is good for a man to listen.

'After the prince had heard the story, he said to me, his capable follower: "Do not play the know-it-all, my friend. Who actually gives water to a bird at dawn, if it is already destined to be slaughtered in the morning?"'

# The Semna Stele from the Sixteenth Year of the Reign of King Senwosret III

*Andreas Hutterer*

Long live the Horus Netjeri-kheperu, Two-Ladies Netjeri-Kheperu-mesut, the king of Upper and Lower Egypt Khai-kau-Re, life may be given to him, long live the golden falcon Kheper, the favourite son of Re of his body, the lord of the two lands, Senwosret, life, prosperity and health to him eternally.

Sixteenth year of the reign, third month of the *peret* season. Establishment of the southern border near Heh through His Majesty.

'I have established my borders by penetrating further south than my forefathers. I multiplied that which had been bequeathed to me.

'I am a king who not only talks, but also acts. What my mind conceives is carried out by my arm. I am a king who attacks to conquer, who acts with determination in order to be successful. Someone who does not tire if a task is in his heart. Someone who gives consideration to the petitioner, who champions the mild-mannered, but who is not lenient against his enemy attacking him but attacks when he himself is attacked. Someone who restrains himself when the other keeps calm. Someone who reacts appropriately to a situation.

'For failure to act after an attack means to strengthen the morale of the enemy. Attack is bravery, retreat a disgrace. A true coward is the one who is driven from his border. For the listening of a Nubian is directed to the trait to fall into despondency solely on the basis of an utterance. To answer him means already to make him retreat. If one proceeds against him, he flees. Yet if one retreats, he prepares to attack. They are no people deserving respect. They are wretched ones, with broken courage.

'My Majesty has seen it, it is thus not a mere allegation. I captured their women and seized their subjects who had gone out to their wells, after their cattle had been slaughtered, their grain uprooted and fire had been lit.

'As truly as my father lives for me, I speak the truth. There are no boastful statements in the words I have said.

'Now concerning each of my successors who will consolidate this border that My Majesty has established. He is my son, he is born to My Majesty. For this is an ideal image of a son who protects his father and consolidates the border of his sire. Yet concerning the one who will give it up and will not fight for it: he is not my son, he is not born to me.

'Furthermore, My Majesty has had a statue of My Majesty made at this border established by My Majesty, so that you (probably meaning the sons) may be safe through it and may fight for it.'

# The Tale of Two Brothers

## Nadine Gräßler

Concerning this, so it is said, there were two brothers of one mother and one father. Anubis, the older brother, had a house and a wife, whereby his younger brother, Bata, was with him in the manner of a son, since he was the one making clothes for him, while he drove his cattle to the fields. He was the one ploughing, the one harvesting for him. He was the one performing all tasks arising in the fields for him.

Now, his younger brother became a perfect man. There was not his equal in the entire land, as the power of god was in him.

After several days his younger brother was herding his cattle as every day. And at the time of evening he returned to his house laden with all herbs of the field, with milk, with wood and with every good product of the field. He laid everything before his elder brother, while the latter sat together with his wife. Then he ate and drank and he in his stable amongst his cattle.

After the land had become light and the next day had come about cooked and laid them before his elder brother. The latter gave him bread loaves for the field, and Bata fetched his cattle to let it graze in the field. He followed his cattle and they spoke to him. 'Good are the herbs in this particular place.' He heard everything they said and took them to the good place for the herbs they desired. And the cattle under his care turned out magnificently and increased their calves considerably.

At the time of ploughing his elder brother said to him: 'Arrange that a team for ploughing is made ready for us, since the field has emerged [from the inundation] so that it is suitable for ploughing. Furthermore, you shall come to the field with the seed, as tomorrow we will begin to plough,' so he said to him.

Thereupon his younger brother made all the arrangements of which his elder brother said to him. 'Do it!' And after the land had become light and the next day had come about, they went to the field with their seed. They started to plough while their hearts were exceedingly delighted with the course of their labour since its commencement.

Several days later they were in the field and they lacked seed. Thereon he sent his younger brother with the words: 'Make haste and fetch us seed from the village.'

And his younger brother found the wife of his elder brother while she was in the process of having her hair done. He said to her: 'Stand up and give me seed, so that I can hasten back to the field, as because of me my elder brother is waiting. Do not allow any delay!'

Then she said to him: 'Go and open the granary. Fetch yourself what you want. Do not let my hair be unfinished.' Thereupon the young man entered his stable and fetched a large *hen* pot, as he wished to pick up much seed. He filled it with barley and wheat and stepped outside with it. She said to him: 'What is the weight on your shoulders?'

And he spoke to her: 'Three sacks of wheat and two sacks of barley, in total five, are upon my shoulders.'

Then she him with the words: 'There is great strength in you. Indeed, I see your strength every day.' And she wished to know him as a man. Then she rose and clung to him. She said to him: 'Come, we want to sleep together for an hour. This will be useful for you, as I will make beautiful garments for you.'

Thereupon the young man became angry like a leopard because of the evil offer she uttered in his presence. And she was fearful beyond all measure. The he talked to her in the following manner: 'Look, you are indeed like a mother to me and your husband like a father. The one older than me, he is actually the one who has raised me. What is the point of this great sin of which you have spoken? Do not speak of it again to me. And I will not tell it to nobody, since I will not let it emerge from my mouth to any person.' He took his load and went to the field by himself. Then he reached his elder brother, and they resumed the performance of their labour.

When evening fell his elder brother returned to his house, while his younger brother continued to herd his cattle. He loaded himself with

36

all products of the field and drove the cattle before him to let it sleep in the stable located in the settlement.

The wife of his elder brother, however, was in fear because of the offer she had uttered. And she fetched fat and bandages and turned herself into someone unjustly beaten for the purpose to say to her husband: 'Your younger brother was the one who has beaten me.' Her husband returned every day in the evening. He reached his house and found his wife who was already faking her sickness, since she did not pour water over his hand as usual and had not lit a light for him either, because of which his house was in darkness while she was vomitting.

Thereon her husband said to her: 'Who was it who spoke to you?'

Then she answered him: 'Nobody talked to me apart from your younger brother, when he came to fetch seed for you. He found me sitting alone. He said to me: "Come, let us sleep together for an hour. You shall let your hair down." But I did not listen to him. "Am I not like your mother? And your elder brother is indeed like a father to you." He became fearful and beat me to prevent my report to you. Yet if you let him live, then I myself will die. Look, when he comes … For I suffer from this evil offer he made during the day.'

Thereon the older brother became like a leopard. He let his spear be sharpened and took it in his hand. The older brother positioned himself behind the gate of his stable in order to kill his younger brother during his return in the evening, as soon as he would let the cattle enter the stable. When the sun went down, Bata loaded himself like every day with all herbs of the field and returned.

The leader cow entered the stable and said to its herdsman: 'Your elder brother is standing in front of you with his spear to kill you. You should flee before him.'

He heard what his leader cow said, and another entered and said the same to him. He looked underneath the gate of the stable and saw the feet of his elder brother, who was standing behind the gate and holding his spear in his hand. He put his load onto the ground and began to hasten to flee, while his brother ran after him with his spear.

His younger brother invoked Re-Horakhty: 'My good lord. You are the one separating lie from truth.' In reply Re answered all his pleas and Re let a great water arise between him and his elder brother filled with crocodiles. So one of them was on one side, while the other was on the other side. His elder brother struck his own hand twice because he had not killed him. Then his younger brother called to him from the other side: "Stay there until morning. When the sun rises, I will litigate with you in its presence. And it will separate the lie from the truth, for I will never again be here with you. I will not be in the place where you are, as I will go to the valley of the pine.'

After the land had become light and the next day had come about, Re-Horakhty rose and one looked upon the other. Then the young man spoke to his elder brother with the words: 'Why are you coming after me in order to kill unjustly without listening to the utterance of my mouth? I am after all your younger brother. And you are to me like a father and your wife is to me like a mother. Was it not so that you had sent me to fetch seed for us, when your wife spoke to me: "Come, let us sleep together for an hour,"'? But look, it was twisted for you into something else.' And he let him know all the things having happened between him and his wife.

Then he swore to him by Re-Horakhty with the words: 'Concerning your arrival to kill me unjustifiably: you carry your spear because of the sex of this immoral woman?' And he took a reed knife and cut off his member. He threw it into the water and a catfish swallowed it. Then he became weak and he felt miserable. His elder brother suffered much in his heart, and he began to lament loudly about him without knowing how to cross to where his younger brother was because of the crocodiles.

Then his younger brother called the following to him: 'If you can remember something bad, are you not able to recall something good too? Or anything I have done for you? Alas, you shall return to your house and take care of your cattle yourself, for I will not remain at the place where you are. I myself will go to the valley of the pine. Yet concerning that which you shall do for me: you shall come to aid me, when you find out that something has happened to me. For I will remove my heart and place it on top of the pine blossom. Yet if the pine is felled, and it falls to the ground, and you come to look for it, even if you spent seven years in the search for it, let your heart not become weary. If, however, you find it and put it in a bowl with cool water, then I will live once more so that I shall avenge the evil done to me. You will know that something has happened to me when a jug of beer is given to you and it foams over. Then do not let yourself be delayed, if this happens to you.'

Then he himself went to the valley of the pine, while his elder brother went to his house. Anubis' hand was on his head and he was smeared with soil. When he reached his house, he killed his wife and fed her to the dogs. Then he sat there in mourning for his younger brother.

After several days his younger brother found himself in the valley of the pine without anybody being with him. He spent the day hunting desert game, and in the evening he came to sleep under the pine, on whose blossom tip his heart was placed. Many days later, he built for himself a castle in the valley of the pine filled with all good things because of his desire to found a house for himself.

When he left the castle, he encountered the divine ennead while they walked about and made decisions for their entire country. Thereat the divine ennead spoke with each other and they said to him: 'Hey, Bata, bull of the divine ennead. Are you all alone here, after you have left your town because of the wife of Anubis, your elder brother? Behold, his wife has been killed. Therewith you have called him to account for all the evil against you.' And their hearts suffered much for him.

Re-Horakhty said to Khnum: 'Please, you should create a wife for Bata so that he does not live alone.' Then Khnum made a companion for him. She was more beautiful in all her limbs than every woman in the entire land, as every god was in her.

Thereupon the seven Hathors approached to see her and they said in unison: 'She will die by a knife.'

Thereon he desired her much. She lived in his house, while he spent the day hunting desert game, bringing it along and presenting it to her. He said to her: 'Do not go outside so that the sea does not seize you. I cannot save you from it, for I am like a woman of your kind. For my heart lies on top of the pine blossom. Yet if another finds it, I will do battle with him.' Then he opened his heart with all its facets to her.

Many days later, Bata went away to hunt as usual. The young woman went out to walk about under the pine beside her house. Thereupon the sea caught sight of her and drove after her. She began to run away from it by entering her house. Thereat the sea called to

39

the pine: 'Seize her for me! And the pine brought a lock of her hair. Then the sea washed it to Egypt and put it at the place of the washermen of the pharaoh – life, prosperity, health.

Thereon the fragrance of the lock of hair arose in the clothes of the pharaoh – life, prosperity, health – and the pharaoh berated the washermen of the pharaoh – life, prosperity, health – with the words: 'The smell of ointment is in the clothes of the pharaoh – life, prosperity, health.' And the pharaoh ranted and raved at them every day without them knowing what to do.

The overseer of the washermen of the pharaoh – life, prosperity, health – ran to the embankment, while his heart was very heavy because of the daily berating of him. Then he stopped and stood on a hill beside the lock of hair in the water. He let them descend and they brought it to him. He found the fragrance very pleasant and took it along for the pharaoh – life, prosperity, health.

Thereupon the knowledgeable scribes of the pharaoh – life, prosperity, health – were fetched and they spoke to the pharaoh – life, prosperity, health: 'This lock of hair, it belongs to a daughter of Re-Horakhty in whom is the seed of each and every god. She is probably a gift for you from another country. Let messengers travel to every foreign land to look for her. Concerning the messenger, however, who will go to the valley of the pine: let many men travel with him in order to fetch her.'

Thereat His Majesty replied – life, prosperity, health: 'Very agreeable is that what you have said.' And they were allowed to leave.

After many days had passed, the men who had travelled to the foreign lands returned to report to His Majesty – life, prosperity, health. Yet those who had gone to the valley of the pine did not return, for Bata had killed them. Only one of them he spared so that he could report to His Majesty – life, prosperity, health. Thereat His Majesty – life, prosperity, health – once more let go forth many soldiers plus charioteers to fetch her. At the same time a woman accompanied those in whose hands were placed all beautiful adornment of women. Thereupon the woman [Bata's wife] came together with her to Egypt, and she was acclaimed in the entire country. Thereon His Majesty – life, prosperity, health – loved her very much, and the pharaoh appointed her great noblewoman. Then he talked to her to let her speak about the peculiarities of her husband.

She said to His Majesty – life, prosperity, health: 'Arrange that the pine is felled and hacked into pieces.' He let go forth soldiers with their tools to fell the pine. They reached the pine and cut off the blossom on top of which Bata's heart was placed. And in this moment Bata fell dead.

Yet when the land had become light and the next day had come about, after the pine had been felled, Anubis, Bata's elder brother, entered his house. He started to wash his hands. He was given a jug of beer, which was foaming over. He was given another one with wine turning sour. Thereupon he took his staff and his sandals as well as his clothes and his weapons. He set off to march to the valley of the pine. He entered the castle of his younger brother and found him lying dead on his bed. Thereon he cried when he saw his younger brother in the state of death. He went off to look for the heart of his younger brother under the pine, under which his younger brother had slept in the evening. He spent three years looking without finding it. Yet when the fourth year began, his heart desired much to return to Egypt. He said: 'I will set off tomorrow.'

After the land had become light and the next day had come about, he began to walk about under the pine. He spent the day looking for the heart and returned in the evening. He once more spent a moment looking for it and meanwhile found a grape and returned with it. Well, this was the heart of his younger brother. He fetched a bowl with cool water, threw the grape into it and sat down as every day. After night had fallen, the heart soaked up the water. Bata trembled in all his limbs. He began to look at his elder brother, while his heart was still lying in the bowl. Anubis, his elder brother, seized the bowl with cool water, in which the heart of his younger brother was found. And he let him drink it. Hereat his heart settled in its place, and he became once more as he had been. Then they embraced each other and talked together.

Thereon Bata said to his elder brother: 'Look, I will turn myself into a large bull with all beautiful colours, the like of which is not known. You shall sit on my back until the sun rises. We will be there where my wife is found so that I can avenge myself. You will take me there where the pharaoh is, and all good things will be done for you, for you will receive my weight in silver and gold because you have brought me to the pharaoh – life, prosperity, health. I will be a great miracle and I will be acclaimed in the entire land. And you shall then leave again for your village.'

After the land had become light and the next day had come about, Bata took on the form he had mentioned to his elder brother. Anubis sat on his back until dawn. He arrived at the place of the pharaoh and His Majesty – life, prosperity, health – was informed about him. He caught sight of him and began to be exceedingly glad about him. He performed a great offering for him with the words: 'This is a great miracle happening.' And he was acclaimed in the entire land. Then he was valued his weight in silver and gold for his elder brother and the latter settled in his village. Many people and many things were given to him and the pharaoh – life, prosperity, health – loved him much more than any other person in the entire land.

Several days later Bata entered the work room and placed himself there, where the noblewoman was. He began to talk to her in the following manner: 'Look, I am still alive.'

She said to him: 'And who are you?'

And he said to her: 'I am Bata. You know, when you had arranged to fell the pine for the pharaoh – life, prosperity, health – this was because of me, to prevent me staying alive. Yet look, I am still alive. I am now a bull.'

Hereat the noblewoman was very fearful because of the news given to her by her husband. Thereupon he left the work room. His Majesty – life, prosperity, health – set out to spend a beautiful day with her.

She poured a drink for His Majesty – life, prosperity, health – and the pharaoh felt very happy in her company. Then she said to His Majesty – life, prosperity, health: 'Swear to me by god with the words: "Concerning that which she will tell him, I will grant it to her."'

And he listened to all she said; 'Oh, let me eat of the liver of this bull, for he will do nothing useful any more.'

Thereon the pharaoh suffered much because of what she had said, and the pharaoh's heart – life, prosperity, health – hurt beyond all measure.

After the land had become light and the next day had dawned, a great offering feast was proclaimed in honour of the bull's sacrifice.

The pharaoh let a first royal servant of His Majesty – life, prosperity, health – go forth to arrange the bull's sacrifice. After that he was allowed to be sacrificed. Yet when he was on the shoulders of the men, he trembled in his neck and let two drops of blood fall beside the two door posts of His Majesty – life, prosperity, health. One of the drops reached one side of the great gate of the pharaoh – life, prosperity, health – while the other reached the other side. They grew into two tall persea trees, each of them being first class.

Thereupon they set off to report to His Majesty – life, prosperity, health: 'Two tall persea trees have grown as a great miracle for His Majesty – life, prosperity, health – during this night on either side of the great gate of His Majesty – life, prosperity, health.' Hereat they rejoiced about them in the entire land, and the pharaoh presented an offering to them.

Many days later, His Majesty – life, prosperity, health – came out to the lapis lazuli window of appearance, wearing a wreath of onions and of all kinds of flowers around his neck. He mounted a chariot of electrum and drove out of the palace to see the persea trees. Then the noblewoman followed on a chariot behind the pharaoh – life, prosperity, health. His Majesty – life, prosperity, health – sat down under one of the persea trees.

Hereat Bata talked to his wife: 'Hey, liar! I am Bata. I am alive in spite of you. You know when you arranged that the pine was felled for the pharaoh – life, prosperity, health – this was because of me. I became a bull and you let me be killed.'

Yet after several days the noblewoman began to pour a drink for His Majesty – life, prosperity, health – and the pharaoh felt happy in her company. She said to His Majesty – life, prosperity, health: 'Swear to me by god with the words: "Concerning this which the noblewoman will say to him, I will grant it to her." So you shall say.' And he listened to all she said.

She spoke: 'Let these two persea trees be felled and made into beautiful furniture.' After a short moment His Majesty – life, prosperity, health – arranged for expert craftsmen to go forth, and the persea trees were felled for the pharaoh – life, prosperity, health. The royal wife, the noblewoman, watched it. Hereat a wooden splinter flew up and penetrated the noblewoman's mouth. She swallowed it and

43

became pregnant immediately. And pharaoh let everything she wished be made out of them.

Many days later she bore a son. They set off to report to His Majesty – life, prosperity, health: 'A son was born to you.' Hereat he was fetched. A wet nurse and other nurses were allocated to him. The entire land rejoiced and the pharaoh set about to celebrate a beautiful day. Thereupon his upbringing commenced. His Majesty – life, prosperity, health – loved him very much from this hour forth and appointed him king's son of Kush. And after several days had passed, His Majesty – life, prosperity, health – made him crown prince of the entire country.

After many days had passed, he had fulfilled many years as crown prince of the entire country. Thereon His Majesty – life, prosperity, health – ascended to the sky. Then Bata said (who is now the new pharaoh): 'Fetch me my high officials of His Majesty – life, prosperity, health – so that I can let them know all matters having happened to me.' And his wife was brought to him, too, with whom he went to court in front of them, whereby they agreed with him. Then his elder brother was brought to him and was appointed crown prince of the entire country. He spent thirty years as king of Egypt. He passed from life, and his elder brother took his place on the day of landing.

It is well and has come to its conclusion in peace for the benefit of the scribe of Pharaoh's treasury – life, prosperity, health – Kagab, the scribe Hori and the scribe Meremope. Made by the scribe Inena, the owner of this script. Concerning him who will speak badly of this script: Thoth will be his adversary.

# Ancient Egyptian Love Poems

## *Renate Fellinger*

### Beginning of the sayings of the great female entertainer/ The walk

(Boy) Unique is the beloved, without her equal,
more beautiful than all other women.
Behold, she is like the goddess of the stars
who rises at the beginning of a good year,
whose skin tone is gleaming, who is magnificent and radiant.
Beautiful are the eyes gazing into the distance,
sweet are her lips talking,
but her speech is not in excess.
With tall neck and glowing bust,
of real lapis lazuli is her hair.
Her arm surpasses gold,
her fingers are like lotus flowers.
With wide hips and narrow waist,
her thighs enhance her beauty.
With steady tread she roams the earth.
She has captured my heart in her embrace.
She causes the heads of all men to turn
at her sight.
Each of her embraces is joy
and he is like the foremost of lovers.
Behold, she steps outside
like this Unique One.

(Girl) The lover has bewitched my heart
with his voice.
He causes me to be smitten by an ailment.
He is one of the neighbours of my mother's house,
but I will not be able to go to him.
Mother is right when she orders me:

"Stop seeing him!"
Behold, my heart is reluctant when I think of him,
his love has captured me.
Behold, he is like one without a heart,
but I am entirely like him.
He does not know my longing to embrace him,
and he does not send anything to my mother.
Beloved, I am awarded to you
by the Golden One among women.
Come to me so that I see your beauty.
Father and mother will rejoice,
all my relatives together
will admire you,
they will hail you, beloved.

(Boy) My heart anticipates
to see her beauty,
while I am sitting idle at home.
I have met Mehi in his chariot
on the street
together with his crowd of lovers.
I will not be able
to behave in his presence,
but I will pass him unimpeded.
Behold, the river is like a street
and I do not know where my feet will carry me.
My heart is becoming more and more ignorant:
"Why are you passing Mehi unimpeded?"
Behold, if I pass him,
I will betray my feelings to him:
"Behold, I belong to you," I will tell him.
Then he will boast with my name
and he will assign me to the foremost group of the seduced
serving him.

(Girl) My heart flees quickly,
when I am thinking of your love.

It does not permit me
to walk like a normal person,
it has leapt from its proper place.
It does not permit me to put on the dress,
I cannot throw the cloak over myself,
I cannot paint my eyes,
I cannot even anoint myself.
"Do not halt until you reach the goal!"
it says to me, whenever I think of him.
Do not be foolish to me, my heart!
Why do you behave so silly?
Sit down and calm yourself!
The lover will come to you
and equally the eyes of many.
Do not let the people talk about me:
"This woman has become weak because of love."
Be steadfast whenever you think of him,
my heart, and do not flee!

(Boy) I will praise the Golden One,
I will honour Her Majesty,
I will glorify the Lady of Heaven,
I will pray to Hathor
and praise the mistress.
I will report to her
so that she answers my prayers
and may award me a lover.
She has come of her own accord to see me.
How beautiful is that which is happening to me!
I am glad and happy and feel splendid,
when they say: "Hey, look, she is here."
Behold, when she comes,
the lovers will kneel before her
due to the power of her love.
I will pray to my Goddess
so that she awards me my beloved as a present.
Three days have passed

since my prayers in her name,
but she has left me five days ago.

(Girl) I went for a walk
in the neighbourhood of his house
and I found its door open.
The beloved stood next to his mother
and all his siblings were with him.
His love captures the hearts of all those
who walk on the street.
An excellent boy without his equal,
a lover of noble character.
When I was passing, he looked at me.
I was by myself and rejoiced.
How happy is my heart with joy,
beloved, since you have noticed me.
If only Mother knew my heart,
she herself would enter at the right time.
Oh Golden One of elation, put it in her heart!
Then I will hasten to my beloved
and will kiss him in front of his friends.
I will not be embarrassed because of the people,
but I will take joy in their knowledge
that you know me.
I will prepare feasts for my Goddess.
My heart leaps and leaves
to arrange that I will see
my beloved tonight.
How wonderful it is to pass!

(Boy) For seven days I have not seen
the beloved,
an ailment has befallen me,
my limbs are heavy,
and I have forgotten myself.
When the physicians come to me,
my heart can find no peace
in their medicines.

The lector priests do not know any treatment, either,
my ailment cannot be diagnosed.
The announcement: "Look, she is here!" revives me,
her name raises me up,
the coming and going of her messengers
stimulates my heart.
The beloved is more important to me
than any medication,
she has more power than the collection of magic spells.
My wellbeing is her entrance.
If I see her, I will be better,
if she opens her eyes,
my body will rejuvenate itself,
if she speaks, I will be strong,
if I embrace her, she will ward off evil from me.
Yet she has left me seven days ago.

**Three wishes**
(Girl) If you only hastened to the beloved
like a swift royal messenger
whose news is desired by the lord
because he wishes to hear them.
All stables are at his command,
horses await him at their resting places,
a chariot is ready at its place
because he is not allowed to stop on the way.
When he has reached the house of the beloved
his heart cheers in joy.

(Girl) If you only hastened to the beloved
like a royal horse,
chosen among a thousand horses of all kinds,
the best of the stables.
It is excellent due to its feed,
and his master recognises its step.
If it hears the cracking of the whip,
it cannot canter slowly.

49

There is no better one among the enemy's troops
which could overtake it.
The heart of the beloved knows
that it is not far from her.

(Girl) If you only hastened to the beloved
like a gazelle leaping across the desert.
Its legs are straying and its body is exhausted,
fear has entered its body.
A hunter pursues it,
accompanied by a dog,
but they cannot even see its dust cloud.
It regards rest like a thorny shrub
and takes the river as its route.
You have reached her cave,
so that your hand may be kissed four times.
You desire the love of the paramour,
the Golden One has awarded her to you, my friend.

**Beginning of the sweet saying found in a book wrapping**
**and which the scribe of the necropolis Nakhtsobek has composed**
(Boy) How skilled is the beloved
at casting the trap,
although no cattle breeder has sired her.
She will cast her hair like a trap towards me,
with her eyes she will capture me,
with her necklace she will bind me
and she brands me with her seal.

(Girl) While you talk to your heart:
"After her! Her embrace is mine."
By Amun, I am the one coming to you,
my dress on my shoulder.

(Boy) What has the beloved done to me!
Shall I remain silent before her regarding this?
She let me stand in front of the door of her house,

while she herself entered.
She did not say to me: "Arrive home safely!"
And she did not spend the night with me.

(Boy) I passed her house in the darkness,
I knocked, but nobody opened for me.
The night is good for our gatekeeper.
Door bolt, I will open you.
Door, you are my destiny.
Are you the spirit belonging to me?
Our ox is slaughtered inside.
Door, do not exercise your power.
Oxen shall be sacrificed for the door bolt,
cattle for the lock,
a fat goose for the door posts
and a bird for the key.
All choice cuts of our ox
are for the Creator of arts,
so that he may build a door bolt of reed
and a door of straw for us.
Any time the lover might come,
he will find her house open
and beds covered with finest linen.
A fair and beautiful girl will stand beside it
and the girl will say to me:
"This house is for the mayor's son."

### Untitled
(Boy) I am sailing downstream on the canal
as a rower of the captain,
my reed bundle is on my shoulder.
I travel to Memphis
and I will say to Ptah,
the Lord of Truth:
"Give me the beloved tonight!"
The river is of wine,
its reed is Ptah,

51

its lotus petal is Sekhmet,
its lotus bud is Iadetyt,
its lotus flower is Nefertem.
… is joy.
The land shines through her beauty.
Memphis is a bowl filled with love apples,
presented to the Gracious One.

(Boy) I will lay down inside
and pretend to be ill.
Then my neighbours will enter to visit
and the beloved will come with them.
She will make the doctors superfluous
because she knows my ailment.

(Boy) The country estate of the beloved,
her door is in the middle of her house,
her gates stand open,
her door bolt is drawn back
and the beloved is furious.
If only I were appointed as gatekeeper,
so I would arrange that she would be angry with me.
Then I would hear her voice when she is angry,
and I would be a child in terror of her.

(Girl) I am sailing downstream
on the canal of the Ruler
and have entered the canal of Re.
My desire is to go
and pitch the tents
near the mouth of the canal in Heliopolis.
I will begin to run
and I will not stop.
My heart will think of Re.
Then I will see the arrival of the beloved,
when he goes to the …
I stand at your side

near the mouth of the canal in Heliopolis.
You have abducted my heart to Heliopolis
and I have retreated with you
to the trees of …
I will harvest the trees of …
which I will use as my fan,
and I will observe what he will do.
My face is directed towards the garden,
my chest filled
with the fruits of the persea tree,
my hair is enriched with balm.
I am the noblewoman of the Lord of the Two Lands,
I …

**Beginning of the entertainment song**
(Girl) The voice of the goose clamours loudly,
as it is caught by its bait.
Your love drives me away,
I cannot release it.
I will take my nets.
What shall I say only to mother,
to whom I go daily
laden with fowl?
The trap was not set today
because I have captured your love.

(Girl) I go away from …
… your love.
May my heart be still inside me.
When I see a sweet cake,
it is as if I saw salt.
Liqueur tasting sweet in my mouth
is like bird's gall.
Only your kiss
revives my heart.
I have found what Amun has given to me,
for ever and ever.

(Girl) The voice of the swallow speaks, it says:
"A new day is dawning,
which is your way?"
Stop it, bird,
you are admonishing me.
I have found the beloved
in his bedroom,
my heart was overjoyed.
We have said:
"I will not be far from you.
My hand will be in your hand,
when I go for a walk with you
in every beautiful place."
He has chosen me as the foremost of the beautiful
and he has not hurt my heart.

(Girl) It is the entrance
to which I turn my face.
Behold, the beloved comes to me.
The eyes are directed towards the street,
my ear strains to listen
because I wait for the idler.
I have chosen the love of the paramour
as my matter alone.
Regarding him
my heart will not be silent.
He has sent me a messenger,
swiftly on foot in coming and going,
to tell me that he has deceived me.
In other words:
he has found another
and she contemplates his face.
What does it matter?
The hurting of another's heart
and the transformation into a stranger.

**Beginning of the [second] entertainment song**
(Girl) The portulaca.

My heart is equal to you.
I will do for you what it desires,
when I lie in your arms.
My prayer paints my eyes,
to see you is the gleaming of my eyes.
I have approached you
to catch sight of your love,
prince of my heart!
How beautiful is my hour,
it turns into eternity for me,
since I have slept with you.
You have lifted my heart
in sorrow and in joy.
Do not leave me.

(Girl) There is monk's pepper
by which one is elevated.
I am your first lover,
I belong to you like the field
which was planted for me with flowers
and with herbs of all manner, sweet in fragrances.
Pleasant is the diked canal
which your hand has dug.
We cool ourselves in the northern wind.
A good place for a walk,
while your hand is lying on top of mine.
My body is cheerful,
my heart rejoices
that we are going for a walk together.
To hear your voice is like liqueur,
I will live because I listen to it.
To see you with each glance
would be better for me
than eating and drinking.

(Girl) There is thyme.
I will take your wreaths,

when you return home drunk.
You will settle down in your bedroom
and I will touch your feet,
while the children … your …
… gladden in …
… health and life inside you …

## The arboretum/arboretum songs
… its …
"My kennels resemble her teeth,
my fruits her breasts.
… of the arboretum.
I am steadfast in each season
which the beloved spends with her lover.
… my …
while they get drunk on wine and liqueur,
who are anointed with the oil of the moringa tree and balm.
All … pass away in the field,
apart from me.
I am spending twelve months in the arboretum,
I am standing and shedding my blossoms,
those of next year are already inside me.
I am the first among my comrades,
but am regarded by them as second rate.
If it is repeated once again,
I will not be silent for their sake.
I will tell it to her friend,
her crime will be uncovered
and the beloved will be punished
so that she will not wind her staffs
with blossoming lotus flowers,
of … of lotus buds,
sweet balm … beer
of all kinds."
She lets you spend the day happily,
a house of reed is the place of the guard.
And behold, it has truly come forth.

Come to us and flatter him,
let him arrange the entire day
because he will otherwise destroy his shelter.

When the fig tree opens its mouth,
its fruit begins to talk:
"let … I have done …
I … to the mistress.
Is there anyone as magnificent as me?
While you have no servants,
I am the servant who ...
as a prize for the beloved.
She let me be planted in her arboretum,
but she does not offer to me …
my … to drink.
My body has not been filled
with water from the animal skins.
While they visit me for recreation,
… not drinking.
By my *ka*, beloved,
… you will have your payback."

The little sycamore, which she has planted
with her own hand,
has opened its mouth to speak.
The words coming from its mouth
are overflowing honey.
It is fair and beautiful, its leaves are lovely,
it turns green and is made to blossom.
It is laden with sycamore figs
and ripe sycamore fruits,
it is redder than jasper.
Its leaves are like turquoise,
its quality is like of faience,
its wood has the colour of green feldspar,
the quality of the wood is as of the *bsbs* tree.
It attracts the one not being under its cover

because its shade is cool.
It places a message into the hand
of a little girl,
the daughter of its gardener,
and lets her hasten to the beloved:
"Come and spend a moment
among the young girls.
The field is in its full flower
and a tent and an arbour are erected below me.
Your gardeners are glad and rejoice,
when they see me.
Send your servants to me,
equipped with their tools.
They become intoxicated when running to me,
although they have not even had a drink.
The servants belonging to you
will come carrying their equipment.
They will bring all kinds of beer,
bread of all varieties,
numerous plants of yesterday and today
and any fruit for joy.
Come so that you may spend
the day in happiness,
tomorrow and the day after tomorrow up to three days,
while you are sitting in my shade."
"Her friend is to her right,
while she makes him drunk
and follows that which he says.
The brewing room is in disarray
because of the drunkenness.
She will stay behind with her lover,
their clothes are spread out under me,
the beloved is taking a walk.
I am discreet so that I will not tell
what I have seen.
Not a word I will say!"

**The crossing**
(Boy) The love of the paramour
is there on the other side.
The river is between us,
the high water is torrential in this season
and a crocodile is waiting on the sandbank.
Yet I descended to the water nonetheless
to wade through the high water,
my heart is valiant in the canal.
I have perceived the crocodile as a mouse
and the surface of the water
like the ground under my feet.
It was her love
which made me strong.
She will recite a water spell for me!
I see the heart of my beloved
when she is standing right before me!

(Boy) The beloved has come,
my heart is glad,
my arms are open to embrace her.
My heart is so happy in its place
like a fish in midst its pond.
Night, you are forever mine,
since the lady has come to me!

**Seven wishes**
(Boy) If only I was
her Nubian maid,
her companion in secret.
She fetches her a bowl with love apples …
It is in her hand
while she is taking pleasure.
In other words:
she has given herself to me
with her naked body.

# The Battle Near Megiddo

## Kathrin Gabler

Horus, Strong Bull Khay-em-Waset, Two-Ladies Wakh-nesut-mi-Re-em-Pet, Gold Horus Sekhem-pekhty-Djeser-Khau, king of Upper and Lower Egypt, the lord of the two lands, Men-kheper-Re, bodily son of Re, Djehuti-mes (Tuthmosis III), life may be given to him eternally.

His Majesty ordered to arrange that the victories, which his father Amun gave him, may be recorded in an inscription in the temple that His Majesty has made for his father Amun, because he wished the campaigns in his name to be preserved, as well as the loot His Majesty brought from there, and the tributes of all the foreign lands given to him by his father Re.

Twenty-second year of the reign, fourth month of the *peret* season, twenty-fifth day: His Majesty was in Tja-ru on the first victorious campaign that his father Amun gave him in order to extend the boundaries of Egypt, in strength, in victory, in power and in justice. Yet this was a period of many years in which Retjenu had degenerated into robbery, while everybody fleeced his companion and … Yet it happened at the time of others that the troops there were in the town of Sharuhen, when they started an uprising against His Majesty from Jarsu till the borders of the country.

Twenty-third year of the reign, first month of the *shemu* season, fourth day, day of the coronation festival near the town Mekh-en-pa-kheka, in Gaza, this is its name in Kha-ru. First month of the *shemu* season, fifth day, going forth to this place in strength, in victory, in power and in justice, in order to subjugate that wretched enemy and to extend the boundaries of Egypt, as ordered by his father Amun-Re and … the victory so that he may seize it.

Twenty-third year of the reign, first month of the *shemu* season, sixteenth day, near the town of Ye-khem. His Majesty ordered to hold council with his victorious army: 'That wretched enemy of Kadesh has come and has entered Ma-k-tj (Megiddo). He is now there. He has gathered around himself the princes of all foreign lands that had been subject to Egypt till Naharina … Kha-ru and Qedut, their horses, their soldiers and their baggage train. He (the enemy) said furthermore: "I will remain to fight against His Majesty here in Megiddo." Tell me your opinion ...'

They said to His Majesty: 'Why shall we go by this route, which is rather narrow? It is reported that the enemies are there, standing outside, and that they are rather numerous. Should not horse go behind horse, as soldier and baggage train equally? Shall our advance-guard be already in battle, while the rearguard is still here in Aruna and cannot fight? There are two other routes: one route, look it is advantageous for us, it is coming out towards Ta-aa-na-ka, while the other, look, it leads to the northern way from/to Djef-tj, and we will emerge in the north of Megiddo. Oh, our victorious lord may go against them there in the excellence of his heart. Yet may he not let us go on that inaccessible route.'

Then the orders concerning that wretched enemy were delivered. Repetition of the report on that plan which they had made before:

That which was said to the Majesty of the palace – life, prosperity, health: 'Upon my life, the love of Re, the praise of my father Amun and my nose young in life and endurance. My Majesty will take this route from Aruna. May those of you who wish it go on the route mentioned by you. May those of you who wish to come in the train of His Majesty go on the other route. For they will say among the enemy, the abomination of Re: "Is His Majesty by any chance going on another route? Perhaps he is beginning to fear us!" so they will say.'

They said to His Majesty: 'Your father Amun-Re, lord of the thrones of the two lands, lord of Karnak, may do as Your Majesty wishes. Look, we follow Your Majesty to any place to which Your Majesty will go. A servant is always behind his master.'

His Majesty ordered to arrange the entire army: 'Your victorious lord will secure your march on that route which is rather narrow. Behold, His Majesty has sworn an oath: "I do not cause my victorious army to go forth from this place before My Majesty."' For His Majesty wanted to go forth himself at the head of his army. Every man was informed of his place during the march of horse behind horse, and His victorious Majesty was at the head of his army.

Twenty-third year of the reign, first month of the *shemu* season, nineteenth day, awaking alive in the tent of him who lives, prospers and is healthy, near the town of Aruna. My Majesty marched northwards under the protection of his father Amun-Re, the lord of Karnak, while Wepwawet was in front of me. Re-Horakhty made the heart of my army enduring, my father Monthu strengthened the arm of My Majesty My Majesty.

Emerging from the pass with His Majesty at the head of his army, which was divided into numerous troops, he did not find a single enemy. The southern wing of the army was in Ta-aa-na-ka, the northern wing was at the southern side of the valley of Kin.

Then His Majesty called out on this route: 'Form up! They have fallen.' That wretched enemy, however, fled this route while the army gave praise to the ruler. Marching of His Majesty on His Majesty behind him, while Amun … The army praised the divine power of His Majesty, for he is greater than any other king.

Twenty-third year of the reign, first month of the *shemu* season, twentieth day, the camp of His Majesty was in Aruna, the rearguard of the victorious army of His Majesty was in the vicinity of Aruna, while the advance-guard already had come forth into the valley of Kin. They filled the mouth of this valley.

Then they said before His Majesty – life, prosperity, health: 'Look, His Majesty has come out from the pass with his victorious army and they are filling the valley. May our lord protect the rearguard of his army with his baggage train. If the rearguard comes out to us, then we will fight against these enemies and then we will not think of our army's rearguard.'

Halting of His Majesty out there and protecting the rearguard of his victorious army. Then the scouts finished the emerging on this route, when the shadow was turning. His Majesty reached the south of Megiddo on the bank of the Brook Kin, when the seventh hour of the day had passed. Then the tent of His Majesty was erected there. The entire army received its orders: 'Prepare yourselves and set up your arms, because in the morning we will meet that wretched enemy in battle.'

Then they ... Being satisfied in the tent of him who lives, prospers and is healthy. Taking care of the provisions of the officials, dispensing the vittles of the retainers, positioning the watches of the army saying to them: 'Be steadfast, be steadfast. And be watchful, be watchful.'

Awakening alive in the tent of him who lives, prospers and is healthy. They came to say to His Majesty: 'The surroundings are sound, the southern and northern troops likewise.'

Twenty-third year of the reign, first month of the *shemu* season, twenty-first day, exactly on the day of the festival of renewal. The king has appeared in the morning. His entire army received the order to form battle lines. His Majesty set out in a chariot of electrum, adorned with his weapons of war, like Horus, with strong arm, master of the deed, like Monthu of Thebes, and his father Amun strengthened his arms. The southern wing of His Majesty's army had to the southern flank of the valley of Kin, the northern wing stood until the north-west of Megiddo, while His Majesty was in their middle. Amun was the protection of his body on the battlefield, the strength of Seth in his body. So His Majesty was mighty at the head of his army. When the enemies saw His Majesty, how powerful he was against them, they fled in mobs back to Megiddo with fear on their faces. They left their horses and their chariots of gold and silver behind, and they were pulled up into the city by their clothes, because the inhabitants had closed the city before them. They let down garments to pull them up into the city. Alas, if only the army of His Majesty had not given so much attention to plunder these enemies' possessions, then they could have conquered Megiddo in an instant. The wretched enemy of Kadesh and the (other) wretched enemies dragged themselves up into the city, climbing to reach it. The fear of His Majesty had taken hold of their bodies, their arms were weary. Then his uraeus became powerful over them.

Their horses and chariots of gold and silver were pillaged as spoils of war. Their weapons lay stretched out, like fish in the fold of the net, while the victorious army of His Majesty counted the associated possessions. The tent of that wretched enemy was captured, decorated with silver. Then the entire army rejoiced and gave praise to Amun because of the victory he had given to his son on this day. They cheered His Majesty because of the greatness of his victory. They brought the loot they had taken: hands [cut from slain enemies], prisoners, horses, chariots of gold, silver, and decorated ones together with all their weapons of war.

Then His Majesty gave orders to his army saying: 'Attack valiantly, attack valiantly, my victorious army! Look, according to the command of Re this city has been given to me today. For every prince of all the foreign lands is trapped in its interior. The conquest of Megiddo is like the conquest of a thousand cities. Take it, be strong. Take it, be strong. Look, the land is ...'

... in order to instruct the overseers of the troops, to let every man know his position. They measured this city, enclosed by a moat and surrounded by fresh timbers of all their different fruit trees. His Majesty himself was at the eastern side of this city and guarded it day and night and lay surrounded by a thick wall with its thickness. Its name was Men-kheper-Re, akh-ta-Aamu. Some people were ordered to guard the tent of His Majesty. They were told: 'Be steadfast, be steadfast. And be watchful. Be watchful.'

Then the army of His Majesty let not one of them to come outside over this wall, apart from one who knocks at the door of their fort.

For everything His Majesty has done against this city, against that wretched enemy and his wretched army, has been immortalised on that day in his name. And the names of the overseers of the troops were immortalised on this day as a leather scroll in the temple of Amun.

The princes of this foreign land came, crawling on their bellies, to kiss the ground before the divine might of His Majesty, to beg for breath for their noses, because of the greatness of his sword, because of the greatness of the divine power of Amun against all foreign lands. All the princes who had presented divine power to His Majesty, they came with gifts: silver, gold, lapis lazuli as well as turquoise, and they carried grain, wine, large and small cattle for the army of His Majesty. A single one of the troops among them had travelled south with gifts. Then His Majesty appointed the princes once more to each city.

List of the loot the army of His Majesty had captured in this city of Megiddo:

Three-hundred-and-forty prisoners, eighty-three hands, 2,041 horses, 191 fillies, six stallions, X young horses chariots decorated with gold etc.

# The Tale of the Prince and his Three Fates

*Andrea Kilian*

Concerning this it is said: there was a king to whom no son had been born. After some time His Majesty asked the gods of his time for a son for himself, and they ordered that it was arranged that one should be born to him. In this night he slept with his wife, and she became pregnant. When she had fulfilled the months of her term, a son was born.

When the Hathors came to decide his fate, they spoke: 'He will die through the crocodile, the snake or the dog.' This was heard by the people at the child's side, too, and they repeated it for His Majesty – life, prosperity, health. Hereupon His Majesty's heart – life, prosperity, health – became very, very sad. His Majesty – life, prosperity, health – then ordered that for his son a house of stone was built in the desert. He furnished it with people and with all good things of the palace – life, prosperity, health – and the child did not venture outside.

Now as the boy had grown, he climbed onto the roof of his house and spotted a greyhound behind an adult man walking on the road. He said to his servant who was beside him: "What is this which walks behind the man who is coming on the road?"

He answered him: 'That is a greyhound.'

The boy said to him: 'Arrange that one of its kind is brought to me.'

Thereupon the servant went and reported this to His Majesty – life, prosperity, health – and His Majesty – life, prosperity, health – said: 'Let him be brought a little puppy so that his heart is not sad.' Thereat he was brought a greyhound immediately.

Now as many days had passed and the boy was grown up, he sent to his father saying: 'What is to be achieved while I am sitting here idle? Look, I am subject to the fates. Let me go away so that I can act according to my heart, until the god does this which is in his mind.'

Thereupon a chariot with horses was readied for him, equipped with all kinds of weapons, and he was given a servant as retainer. He was ferried to the eastern bank, and it was said to him: 'May you follow your wish,' and his greyhound was with him. He travelled northwards, following his heart, through the desert, and he lived off the choicest of all desert game.

He reached the prince of Naharina. Now the prince of Naharina had no children except one daughter. For her a house had been built, the window of which was 70 cubits above the ground. He let all the sons of all the princes of the land Khor be fetched and said to them: 'He who reaches the window of my daughter receives her as his wife.'

Now as many days had passed and the sons of the princes were busy with their daily matters, the boy was passing them. Hereat they brought him to their house. They washed him, fed his team of horses and did everything for the boy. They salved him, bound his feet, gave food to his retainer and said to him in a talkative mood: 'From where do you come, handsome boy?'

He said to them: 'I am the son of a charioteer from the land of Egypt. My mother is dead, and my father took another wife, a stepmother. She began to hate me, and I left in flight from her.' They embraced him and kissed him from head to toe.

Now as many days had passed, he said to the sons: 'What is it that you are doing here?'

They said to him: 'For three whole months until today we are passing our time here with jumping. For the one who reaches the window of the prince of Naharina's daughter will take her as his wife.'

He said to them: 'Alas, if only my feet would not hurt so much. Then I would go with you to jump.' They went to jump according to their daily habit. The boy stood at some distance and watched, while the gaze of the prince of Naharina's daughter lay on him.

Now as many days had passed, the boy came to jump together with the sons of the princes. He jumped, and he reached the window of the prince of Naharina's daughter. She kissed him and embraced him from head to toe. Then someone went to please her father's heart by telling

68

him: 'One of the men has reached your daughter's window.'

Thereat the prince questioned him with the words: 'The son of which prince is he?'

He was told: 'A charioteer's son. He has come from the land of Egypt on the run from his stepmother.'

Hereat the prince of Naharina became angry beyond all measure. Then he said: 'Shall I actually give my daughter to this fugitive from Egypt? Let him go away.'

They went to tell him: 'Alas, you shall go where you have come from.'

Hereupon the daughter seized him, swearing by god with the words: 'As Re-Horakhty endures: if he is taken from me, I will not eat or drink, I will die immediately.'

The messenger went and reported to her father all she had said. And her father sent men to kill him on the spot. The daughter said to them: 'By Re, if he is killed, I will die as soon as the sun goes down. I will not live an hour longer than him.' Hereat they went to tell this to her father.

Thereupon her father let the youth be brought before him together with his daughter. The youth stepped before him, and his charisma impressed the prince. He embraced him, kissed him from head to toe and said to him: 'Tell me about yourself, since you are now here with me as my son.'

He told him: 'I am the son of a charioteer from the land of Egypt. My mother is dead, and my father has taken another wife. She began to hate me and I went on the run from her.'

Then he gave him his daughter as the wife. He gave him a house together with fields, likewise cattle and all good things.

Now as many days had passed, the youth said to his wife: 'I am delivered to three fates: the crocodile, the snake and the dog.'

She said to him: 'Let the dog be killed which is following you.'

Yet he replied to her: 'I will not let my dog be killed, which I have raised since it was little.'

And so she began to guard her husband closely and did not let him venture forth alone.

On the day, however, on which the youth had come from the land of Egypt to roam about, the crocodile too, his fate (had followed him).

69

It happened that it was opposite to him (dwelling) in a lake in the village in which the youth was found. Yet a demon was in it too. The demon did not let the crocodile out and the crocodile did not let the demon out to roam, since as soon as the sun rose they started to fight each other, every day for two whole months.

Now as many days had passed, the youth began celebrating in his house. When the night had fallen, the youth lay down on his bed, and sleep took over his body. His wife filled a bowl with wine and another with beer. Then a snake slithered out of its hole to bite the youth, but his wife sat at his side and did not sleep. The bowls attracted the snake. It drank and became tipsy. Then it lay on its back, and his wife let it be hacked into pieces with her axe. After that she woke her husband and said to him: 'Look, your god has given one of your fates in your hand, he will protect you …' He gave an offering to Re while praying to him daily and praising his power.

Now as many days had passed, the youth went out to walk around his estate for pleasure. His wife did not go out with him, but his dog followed him.

Hereat his dog started to talk and said: 'I am your fate.' Hereupon he ran from it. When he reached the lake, he jumped in to the water, in flight from the dog. And so the crocodile seized him and brought him there where the demon was …

The crocodile said to the youth: 'I am your fate that has followed you. Until now I have fought two whole months with the demon. Now look, I will release you if my … to fight  … so you shall praise me. Kill the demon. For if you catch sight … sees the crocodile.

After the land had become light and the next day had begun, came …

End of the manuscript.

# Coptic Magical Texts

*Renate Fellinger*

### pSchmidt I

Listen, Horus is crying,
listen, Horus is sighing.
(Horus:) "I have suffered
because I desired seven virgins
from the third hour of the day
to the forth hour of the night.
None of them slept,
none of them dozed."
His mother Isis answered him
in the temple of Habin,
while her face was directed
to the seven virgins
and the seven virgins were turned
to her face.
(Isis:) "Horus, why are you crying?
Horus, why are you sighing?"
(Horus:) "You want me not to cry,
you want me not to sigh
from the third hour of the day
to the forth hour of the night,
when I am desiring the seven virgins?
None of them slept,
none of them dozed."
(Isis:) "Even though you have not found me,
even though you have not found my name,
take a beaker
with a little water,
either it should be a small breath,

71

the breath of your mouth,
or the breath of your nose.
Invoke over them:
'*pkekhp*...'"
The two angels who brought sleep over *Aftimelekh*
for seventy-two years, placed you onto NN,
son/daughter of NN. You weigh heavy on his
head like a millstone, on his eyes like a sandbag,
until I satisfy my lust and fulfil the desire of my heart,
soon, soon, quickly, quickly!

## pSchmidt II
I am NN, son/daughter of NN,
I went inside through a door of stone
and I came outside through a door of iron.
I went inside with my head first
and I came outside with my feet first.
I found seven virgins
sitting near a source of water.
I lusted, but they desired not.
I persuaded, but they could not be swayed.
I wanted to love NN, the daughter of NN,
but she did not want to receive my kiss.
I fortified myself, I stood upright.
I cried, I sighed,
until the tears of my eyes
covered the soles of my feet.
Isis answered:
"What is the matter with you, man, son of the sun,
that you are crying and sighing
until the tears of your eyes
cover the soles of your feet?"
(Horus:) "Why, Isis, do you not want me to cry?
I went inside through a door of stone
and I came outside through a door of iron.
I went inside with my head first
and I came outside with my feet first.

I found seven virgins
sitting by a source of water.
I lusted, but they desired not.
I persuaded, but they could not be swayed.
I wanted to love NN, the daughter of NN,
but she did not want to receive my kiss."
(Isis:) "Why did you go inside through a door of stone
did come outside through a door of iron,
did find seven virgins
and did lust, but they desired not,
did want to love NN, the daughter of NN,
but she did not want to receive your kiss?
You have not fortified yourself
and have not stood upright,
you have not spoken in seven tongues:
*'thetf'* seven times."
You great one among the spirits,
I want that NN, the daughter of NN,
spends forty days and forty nights
clinging to me,
like a bitch to a dog,
like a sow to a boar.
Then I call,
and you must be ready.

**From Michigan 136**
I invoke you, great Isis,
who rules the absolute blackness,
mistress of the celestial gods from birth onwards,
Atherneklesia, Athernebouni, Labisakhthi,
Khomokhookhi, Isi, Souse, Mounte,
Tntoreo, Iobast, Bastai, Ribat, Khribat, Oeresibat,
Khamarei, Khurithibath, Souere, Thartha,
Thabaaththa, Thath, Bathath, Lathai,
Akhra, Abathai, Ae.
Let the body of NN, born of NN, reach
the state as given by god and be free from

73

inflammation, danger and pain for ever,
now, now, immediately, immediately!
Soak a piece of white wool. Place it under it
(her body) for immediate healing.

### pBerlin 8313, col. II and verso

Jesus! Horus, son of Isis, climbed a mountain
to rest there. He played his music, set up his nets
and caught a falcon, a *bank* bird and a wild pelican.
He cut it up without a knife, cooked it without a fire
and ate it without salt. He was in pain,
the area around his navel was hurting him, and
he cried, loudly wailing: "Today I fetch myself
my mother Isis. I want a demon so that
I can send him to my mother Isis."
The first demon Agrippas came to him and said:
"Do you want to go to your mother Isis?"
He (Horus) said: "How long will you take
to go there and come back again?
He (Agrippas) spoke: "How long will you take
to go there and come back again? I can
go there in two hours and can be back again in two hours."
He (Horus) said: "Go away, you do not suffice me!"
The second demon Agrippas came to him and said:
"Do you want to go to your mother Isis?"
He (Horus) said: "How much time do you need to
go there and come back again?"
He (Agrippas) spoke: "I can go there in one hour
and come back again in another."
He (Horus) said: "Go away, you do not suffice me!"
The third demon Agrippas, the one with only one eye and one hand,
came to him and said:
"Do you want to go to your mother Isis?"
(Horus:) "How long will you need to go there
and come back again?"
(Agrippas:) "I can go there with the breath of your mouth
and come back again with the breath of your nose."

(Horus:) "So go, you satisfy me!"
He climbed the mountain of Heliopolis and found
his mother Isis who wore an iron crown and
stoked a copper kiln. She said to him: "Demon Agrippas,
from where have you come to this place?"
He said to her: "Your son Horus climbed a mountain to rest there.
He played his music, set up his nets
and caught a falcon, a *bank* bird and a wild pelican.
He cut it up without a knife,
cooked it without a fire and ate it without salt. He was in pain
and the area around his navel was hurting him."
She said to him: "Even though you have not found me
and my name, the true name,
which the sun carries to the west and the moon to the east,
and which is carried by the six conciliatory stars under the sun,
you shall invoke the 300 vessels
which are located around the navel:
'Let every illness, every suffering and every pain
which are inside the body of NN, son/daughter of NN
cease immediately. I am the one who calls, Lord Jesus
grants the healing.'"

### London Hay 10434, verso

For NN, son/daughter of NN, Michael, give mercy,
Gabriel, give life. Suriel, give honour. Raphael, give life.
Sebthor, give mercy. Anael, give honour. Bathoriel, give NN,
son/daughter of NN, desire for NN,
son/daughter of NN, all the days of his/her life.

### pBibl. Nat. Suppl. gr. no. 574 (Great Paris Magical Papyrus)/ PGM IV

It is Isis who is climbing down from the mountain at noon during summer, the dusty young woman. Her eyes are filled with tears and her heart is full of sighs. Her father, Thoth, the great, came to her and asked: "My daughter Isis, you dusty young woman, why are your eyes filled with tears and your heart with sighs … your clothing soiled? Away with the tears in your eyes!"

75

She replied to him: "He is not with me, my father, monkey Thoth, monkey Thoth, my father. I was betrayed by my girlfriend. I have discovered a secret: yes, Nephthys is sleeping with Osiris ... my brother, the son of my own mother."

He said to her: "See, that is adultery against you, my daughter Isis."

She replied to him: "It is adultery against you, my father, monkey Thoth, monkey Thoth, my father. It is true conception for myself."

He said to her: "Rise, my daughter Isis, and go south of Thebes and north of Abydos. There are ... those who are stamping about there. Fetch for yourself Belf, son of Belf, whose foot is of bronze and whose heels are of iron, so that he may forge for you a double iron nail with a ... head, ... a thin base, a strong tip and from light iron. Bring it to me, dip it into the blood of Osiris and give it to me. We ... this flame ... to me."

"Each flame, each boiling, each heating up, each steaming, each sweating that you will create in this flame stove, you have to cause in the heart, in the liver, in the area of the navel, inside the body of NN, born of NN, until I bring her to the house of NN, born of NN, and she gives that which is in her hand into my hand, that which is in her mouth into my mouth, that which is inside her body into my body, that which is in her sexual organs into my sexual organs, quickly, quickly, immediately, immediately! Rise and go to the kings of Alkhah and speak the truth in Oupoke, let god desire NN, born of NN, and I will send her to be together with NN, born of NN. As I am To, son of To. I am the great son of the great one. I am Anubis who wears the glorious crown of Re ... and crowns the king Osiris Wennefer with it, ... arousing the entire world so that you may arouse the heart of NN, born of NN, so that I know what is in her heart for me, for NN, born of NN, on this day."

If a large amount of saliva forms in your mouth, while you speak, understand that she is troubled and wants to talk to you. If you are yawning frequently, she wants to come to you. Yet if you sneeze twice or more, she is physically well and will return to where she lives. If you have a headache and are crying, she is disturbed and is perhaps even dying.

"Ascend to the sky and let the Elevated desire the Noble. Ascend to the abyss and let Thoth desire Nabin. Arouse the hearts of these two bulls, Hapi and Mnevis. Let the heart of Osiris desire Isis. Let Re desire the light. Let the heart of NN, born of NN, desire NN, born of NN."

Say these things in the interest of women. Yet if you say them against women, then speak the reverse so that the women desire the men.

"If she drinks, if she eats, if she sleeps with someone else, I will bewitch her heart. I will bewitch her heart, I will becharm her breath, I will entrance her 365 limbs, I will bewitch her innermost ... wherever I want, until she comes to me, and I know what is in her heart, what she is doing and what she is thinking. Quickly, quickly, immediately, immediately!"

# Bibliography

## The Biographical inscription of the Soldier Amenemheb Called Mehu

Blumenthal, Elke/Müller, Ingeborg/Reineke, Walter F. (eds), *Urkunden der 18. Dynasty. Übersetzungen zu den Heften 5-16*, Berlin 1984, p310-313 [268]

Gabriel, Richard A., *Thutmose III. The military biography of Egypt's greatest warrior king*, Washington DC 2009, p159-185

Heye, Heike (formerly Guksch), "Amenemheb und die Hyäne. Norm und Individualität in der Grabdekoration der 18, Dynastie", in: Heike Heye (formerly Guksch)/Eva Hofmann/Martin Bommas (eds), *Grab und Totenkult im Alten Ägypten*, Munich 2003, p104-117

[Note: the tomb of Amenemheb has been examined archaeologically since 1990 by the Institute of Egyptology of the University of Heidelberg, and the publication of the results is currently being prepared by Heike Heye.]

Kampp, Friederike, *Die Thebanische Nekropole. Zum Wandel des Grabgedankens von der XVIII. Bis zur XX. Dynastie (Theben 13)*, part 1, Mainz 1996, p336-338 [TT 85]

Sethe, Kurt, *Urkunden des ägyptischen Altertums. IV. Abteilung, Urkunden der 18. Dynastie. Historisch-biographische Urkunden vol 3*, Berlin 1927/1930 (unaltered reprint Berlin/Graz 1961), p889-897 [no 268]

## The Autobiography of Sinuhe

Blackman, Aylward M., *Middle Egyptian Stories (Bibliotheca Aegyptiaca; vol II/1)*, Brussels 1932, p1-41

Blumenthal, Elke, "Die Erzählung des Sinuhe", in: O. Kaiser et al. (eds): *Weisheitstexte, Mythen und Epen III (TUAT III,5)*, Gütersloh 1995, p884-911

Burkard, Günter/Thissen, Heinz J. "Die Geschichte des Sinuhe", in:

*Einführung in die altägyptische Literaturgeschichte vol. 1, Altes und Mittleres Reich,* Münster 2003, 110-119

Parkinson, Richard B., *The Tale of Sinuhe and Other Ancient Egyptian Poems 1940-1640 BC*, Oxford 1997, p21-53

**The Instructions of King Amenemhat I for his son Senwosret I**

Adrom, Faried, *Die Lehre des Amenemhet (BAE 19)*, Turnhout 2006

Blumenthal, Elke, "Die Lehre des Königs Amenemhet (Part I + II)", in: *Zeitschrift für Ägyptische Sprache und Altertumskunde 111* (1984), p85-107, + *112* (1985), p104-115

Burkard, Günter, "'Als Gott erschienen spricht er.' Die Lehre des Amenemhet als postumes Vermächtnis", in: Jan Assmann/Elke Blumentahl (eds), *Literatur und Politik im pharaonischen und ptolemäischen Ägypten. Vorträge der Tagung zum Gedenken an Georges Posener, 5 – 10. September 1996 in Leipzig (BdE 127)*, Cairo 1999, p153-173

Dils, Peter, "Die Lehre des Amenemhet. Übersetzung und Kommentar", in: *Thesaurus Lingua Aegyptia*: http://aaew.bbaw.de/tla/index.html (last accessed 10/05/2012)

Jansen-Winkeln, Karl, "Das Attentat auf Amenemhet I. und die erste ägyptische Koregentschaft", in: *Studien zur altägyptischen Kultur 18* (1991), p241-264

Lichtheim, Miriam, *Ancient Egyptian Literature. A book of readings. Volume I: The Old and Middle Kingdoms*, Berkeley/ Los Angeles/ London 1973, p135-139

**The Tale of the Shipwrecked Sailor**

Burkard, Günter/Thissen, Heinz J., *Einführung in die altägyptische Literaturgeschichte I. Altes und Mittleres Reich*, Münster/Hamburg/ London 2003

Foster, John L./Brock, Lyla P., *The Shipwrecked Sailor. A Tale from Ancient Egypt*, Cairo/New York 1998

Goedicke, Hans, *Die Geschichte des Schiffbrüchigen (Ägyptologische Abhandlungen 30)*, Wiesbaden 1974

Parkinson, Richard B., *The Tale of Sinuhe and other Ancient Egyptian Poems 1940-1640 BC*, Oxford 1997

## The Semna Stele from the Sixteenth Year of the Reign of King Senwosret III

Delia, Robert D., *A study of the reign of Senwosret III*, New York 1980, p42-77

Eyre, Christopher, "The Semna Stelae. Quotation, genre, and functions of literature", in: Sarah Israelit-Groll (ed), *Studies in Egyptology presented to Miriam Lichtheim*, vol 1, Jerusalem 1990, p134-165

Lichtheim, Miriam, *Ancient Egyptian Literature. A book of readings. Volume 1: The Old and Middle Kingdoms*, Berkeley/Los Angeles/London 1973, p118-120

Seidlmayer, Stephan J., "Zu Fundort und Aufstellungskontext der großen Semna-Stele Sesostris III.", in: *Studien zur altägyptischen Kultur 28* (2000), p233-242

Wildung, Dietrich (compiler), *Sudan. Antike Königreiche am Nil* [exhibition catalogue Munich], Tübingen 1996, p78-79

## The Tale of Two Brothers

Assmann, Jan, "Das ägyptische Zweibrüdermärchen (Papyrus d'Orbiney). Eine Textanalyse auf drei Ebenen am Leitfaden der Einheitsfrage", in: *Zeitschrift für Ägyptische Sprache und Altertumskunde 104* (1977), p1-25

Blumenthal, Elke, "Die Erzählung des Papyrus d'Orbiney als Literaturwerk", in: *Zeitschrift für Ägyptische Sprache und Altertumskunde 99* (1973), p1-17

Gardiner, Alan H., *Late Egyptian Stories (Bibliotheca Aegyptiaca 1)*, Brussels 1932, p9-29

Hollis, Susan Tower, *The Ancient Egyptian "Tale of Two Brothers". A Mythological, Religious, Literary and Historico-Political Study*, Oakville 2008

Peust, Carsten, "Das Zweibrüdermärchen", in: Otto Kaiser (ed), *Texte aus der Umwelt des Alten Testaments*. Supplement, Gütersloh 2001, p147-165

Wettengel, Wolfgang, *Die Erzählung von den beiden Brüdern. Der Papyrus d'Orbiney und die Königsideologie der Ramessiden (Orbis Biblicus et Orientalis 195)*, Fribourg/ Göttingen 2003

## Ancient Egyptian Love Poems

Fox, Michael V., *The Song of Songs and the Ancient Egyptian Love Songs,* Madison 1985

Hermann, Alfred, *Altägyptische Liebesdichtung,* Wiesbaden 1959

Landgráfová, Renata/Navrátilová, Hana, *Sex and the Golden Goddess I. Ancient Egyptian Love Songs in Context,* Prague 2009

Mathieu, Bernard, *La poésie amoureuse de l'Égypte ancienne. Recherches sur un genre littéraire au Nouvel Empire,* Cairo 1996

Schott, Siegfried, *Altägyptische Liebeslieder. Mit Märchen und Liebesgeschichten.* Zurich 1950

White, John Bradley, *A Study of Love in the Song of Songs and Ancient Egyptian Poetry (Society of Biblical Literature. Dissertation Series 38),* Missoula 1978


## The Battle Near Megiddo

Gabriel, Richard A., *Thutmose III. The military biography of Egypt's greatest warrior king,* Washington DC 2009

Goedicke, Hans, *The Battle of Megiddo,* Baltimore 2000

Priese, Karl-Heinz, "Heft 9/10, Historisch-biographische Urkunden aus der Zeit Thutmosis' III., Nr. 201-Nr.215", in: Elke Blumenthal/ Ingeborg Müller/ Walter F. Reineke (eds) *Urkunden der 18. Dynasty. Übersetzungen zu den Heften 5-16,* Berlin 1984, p189-195

Redford, Donald B., *The Wars in Syria and Palestine of Thutmose III. Culture and History of the Ancient Near East, Vol. 16,* Leiden/ Boston 2003

Sethe, Kurt, *Urkunden des ägyptischen Altertums. IV. Abteilung, Urkunden der 18. Dynastie. Historisch-biographische Urkunden vol 2, issue 5, 8-11,* Leipzig 1906/7, p645-664

Sternberg-el Hotabi, Heike, "Aus den Annalen Thutmosis' III.: Erster Feldzug gegen Megiddo", in: Bernd Janowski/ Wilhelm Gernot (eds), *Staatsverträge, Herrscherinschriften und andere Dokumente zur politischen Geschichte. Texte aus der Umwelt des Alten Testaments (TUAT).* New Series vol 2, Gütersloh 2005, p212-220

*Digital Karnak*: http://dlib.etc.ucla.edu/projects/Karnak

*Lepsius Denkmäler online Publikation = Lepsius-Projekt Sachsen Anhalt, LD III 31 b-32* (battle of Megiddo): http://edoc3.bibliothek. uni-halle.de/lepsius/textb.html

**The Tale of the Prince and his Three Fates**

Brunner-Traut, Emma, *Altägyptische Märchen. Mythen und andere volkstümliche Erzählungen,* Munich [11]1997, p55-60

Burkard, Günter/Thissen, Heinz J., *Einführung in die altägyptische Literaturgeschichte II. Neues Reich*, Berlin 2008, p7-18

Lichtheim, Miriam, *Ancient Egyptian Literature. A book of readings. Volume 2: The New Kingdom*, London 1976, p200-203

Wente Jr., Edward F., "The Tale of the Doomed Prince", in: William Kelly Simpson (ed), *The Literature of Ancient Egypt. An Anthology of Stories, Instructions, Stelae, Autobiographies, and Poetry*, New Haven/ London [3]2003, p75-79

**Coptic Magical Texts**

Betz, Hans Dieter (ed), *The Greek Magical Papyri in Translation. Including the Demotic Spells,* Chicago/London 1986

Borghouts, Joris F., *Ancient Egyptian Magical Texts*, Leiden 1978

Kropp, Angelicus M., *Ausgewählte Koptische Zaubertexte,* 3 volumes, Brussels 1930/31

Meyer, Marvin W./Smith, Richard (eds), *Ancient Christian Magic. Coptic Texts of Ritual Power,* Princeton 1994

Pinch, Geraldine, *Magic in Ancient Egypt,* 2nd edition, London 2006

# The Texts

*The bibliographical inscription of the soldier Amenemheb called Mehu* is found on a wall in his tomb in Western Thebes. *The autobiography of Sinuhe* is preserved – though not always in its entirety – both on various papyri and on ostraca. The preserved, incomplete copies (five papyri, three wooden tablets, a leather scroll, more than 300 ostraca) of the *instructions of King Amenemhat I for his son Senwosret I* date to the New Kingdom. *The tale of the shipwrecked sailor* is transmitted on pPetersburg 1115 from the Middle Kingdom and probably originated in the twelfth dynasty. The Semna stele from the sixteenth year of the reign of King Senwosret III is today located in the Egyptian Museum, Berlin. *The tale of two brothers* is recorded in hieratic script in pD'Orbiney and probably dates to the Post-Amarna Period. For the *ancient Egyptian love poems* different cycles of the New Kingdom are compiled – complete (c) or in part (ip): pChester Beatty I verso: *beginning of the sayings of the great female entertainer*, today often titled as *the walk* (c), *three wishes* (modern title; c); pChester Beatty I recto: *beginning of the sweet saying which was found in a book wrapping and which the scribe of the necropolis Nakhtsobek has composed* (ip); pHarris 500 recto: *untitled* (ip), *beginning of the entertainment song* (ip), *beginning of the entertainment song* (c); pTurin 1966 recto: *the arboretum/arboretum songs (c);* oDM 1266 and oCGC 25218: *the crossing, seven wishes* (both ip; modern titles). *The battle near Megiddo* is found in the so-called Annals Hall in the temple complex of Karnak. *The tale of the prince and his three fates* is preserved on the back of pHarris 500 in an incomplete version, which dates to the beginning of the nineteenth dynasty. An excursion in time is represented by the *Coptic magic spells* from the fourth to eight century AD.

# The Authors

*Meike Becker* studied Egyptology in Münster and received her PhD at the Freie University, Berlin in 2010. She participated in excavations in Assiut from 2005. Since 2009 she has been a research fellow at the Institute for Egyptology and Coptology at the Westphalian Wilhelms-University Münster.

*Renate Fellinger* studied Egyptology with a philological specialisation at Cambridge University and obtained an MA with distinction in 2011 with the dissertation "Sex object or equal partner? The role of women as portrayed in the ancient Egyptian love poems". Since autumn 2011 she has been working on her doctoral thesis in the area of ancient Egyptian legal history and gender studies at Cambridge.

*Kathrin Gabler* studied Egyptology, Classical Archaeology and Religious Studies. She is currently a postgraduate research student at the Ludwig-Maximilian-University and has been participating since 2007 in different excavations in Egypt.

*Nadine Gräßler* studied Egyptology and Ancient Oriental Philology. She has worked on excavations in Western Thebes. Today she is a postgraduate research student at the Institute for Egyptology and Ancient Oriental Studies at the Johannes-Gutenberg-University Mainz.

*Anja Hilbig* studied Egyptology, Classical Archaeology and Ancient History at the University of Leipzig and is responsible for the section Egypt in the catalogue accompanying the temporary exhibition "Ex Oriente Lux – Schätze aus Oberlausitzer Privatsammlungen" of the Museum of the Western Lausitz. She is currently participating in the excavation project of the German Archaeological Institute Department Cairo in Dra' Abu el Naga, Egypt.

*Andreas Hutterer* completed his MA in Egyptology in Munich and gained his doctorate in 2011 with the topic "Historical Studies on Amenemhet II". Since 2002 he has been working as research fellow and university teacher at the Institute of Egyptology of the Ludwig-Maximilian-University Munich.

*Andrea Kilian* studied Egyptology, Prehistory and Educational Science in Mainz. She participated in excavations in Western Thebes, and since 2009 has been a research assistant of "The Asyut Project" of the Johannes-Gutenberg-University Mainz funded by the German Research Foundation, and a postgraduate research student.

*Agnes Klische* initially completed training as a special nurse for anaesthesia and intensive-care medicine. This was followed by studies in Archaeology, Protestant Theology and Ancient History in Mainz. Currently, she is working on her doctoral thesis with the working title "Personified representations of sky and earth in ancient Egypt".

# Glossary

Note: Ellipses [...] and NN = These represent a space where the original hieroglyphs is missing and so no accurate translation can be provided

| | |
|---|---|
| *Amun* | Anthropomorphic creator and fertility god based in Thebes who rose to prominence in the Middle Kingdom, when he developed a close connection to the pharaoh as god of the empire; sometimes viewed as king of gods; often joined with other deities such as Re or Min; his name could be translated as 'the hidden one' |
| *Aruna* | Locality in the Levant |
| *Aten* | A description of the sun disc since the Middle Kingdom, Aten becomes a solar god in the eighteenth dynasty. The 'heretic pharaoh' Akhenaten made Aten sole deity in his new theology |
| *Atum* | Anthropomorphic primordial creator god based in Heliopolis |
| *ba* | One of the components of personhood (or of the soul) imminent to deities and humans alike, embodying the imperishable aspects; depicted as a bird with a human head, but being able to take on any form desired |
| *Biga* | Island in the first Nile cataract near Aswan |
| *Byblos* | Modern Gubla, located on the northern coast of the Lebanon; an important trading port since the late fourth millennium BC, around the first millennium it is inhabited by Phoenicians |
| *Djef-ti* | Modern Tell Abu Shushe, 4km north-west of Megiddo |
| *Djeser-akhet* | Name of a temple in Deir el-Bahari (western Thebes) |
| *ennead* | Circle of nine deities whose composition varies from place to place. The concept was first developed in |

|  |  |
|---|---|
|  | Heliopolis, but later transferred to other important cult places such as Memphis and Thebes. It symbolises the entirety of the divine powers ruling the world |
| *Golden falcon = Gold Horus* | One of the five titles of the pharaoh |
| *Hapi* | Hermaphrodite personification of the Nile, or specifically the inundation; also the name of a sacred bull associated with the god Ptah |
| *Haroëris* | Special form of Horus: the 'elder' Horus |
| *Hathor* | Important goddess associated with many aspects, celestial or cosmic, but also of love, sexuality and festive activities, with main seat in Dendera; depicted either as a woman with cow ears and horns or as a cow |
| *Heh* | Egyptian name of modern Abu Sir at the second Nile cataract c 40 km north of Semna, a Middle Kingdom fortress |
| *Horakhty* | 'Horus of the two horizons'; special form of Horus, most often connected to Re |
| *Horus* | Cosmic deity with close association to the king since prehistoric times, i.e. the living king is often identified as Horus; depicted falcon-headed or as a falcon |
| *Horus name* | One of the five titles of the pharaoh, the earliest recorded, dating back to the early fourth millennium BC, frequently used, e.g. on seals and administrative documents |
| *Iadetyt* | Minor goddess in Memphis |
| *Iku* | A quarrying area near Cairo |
| *Imhet* | Necropolis complex between Helwan and Cairo |
| *Ipet* | Annual religious festival in Thebes lasting two to four weeks; main event was the procession of divine images in portable barks from Karnak to Luxor |
| *Isis* | Anthropomorphic goddess of unknown origin, wearing the symbol of a throne on her head. In mythology wife of Osiris and mother of Horus, with mainly protective functions, also closely associated with magic |
| *Jarsu* | Unidentified locality |

| | |
|---|---|
| *ka* | One of the components of personhood (or of the soul) symbolised by two raised arms, associated with physical (procreative) and spiritual strength |
| *Kadesh* | City state on the River Orontes |
| *Ka-Nefer* | Name of the pyramid of Amenemhat I at Lisht in the Fayum |
| *Karkemish* | City state on the western bank of the Euphrates (Turkey) |
| *Kedem* | Area in the Lebanon near Byblos |
| *Kenemtiu* | Inhabitants of the Kharga Oasis in the Libyan Desert |
| *Kharbu* | Locality in the Levant |
| *Khar-ru* | Locality in the Levant |
| *Khenem-Sut* | Name of the mortuary temple of Senwosret I near Lisht in the Fayum |
| *Khentkeshu* | Region near Retjenu |
| *Khnum* | Creator god depicted as a ram or with a ram's head who fashions the human form on a potter's wheel |
| *Khor* | Egyptian name for Syria and Palestine meaning 'land of the Hurrians' |
| *King of Upper and Lower Egypt* | One of the five titles of the pharaoh; frequently used, e.g. together with the son of Re title on monuments in the New Kingdom |
| *King's son of Kush* | Also Viceroy of Kush; an office created in the New Kingdom to govern the part of Nubia under Egyptian control in the pharaoh's stead |
| *Maati* | Canal near Giza |
| *Maryannu* | Name for the people of the Mitanni empire |
| *Medja* | Nomadic group from the eastern desert in Nubia associated with the pan-grave culture; after the Middle Kingdom employed by the Egyptians as scouts and light infantry |
| *Megiddo* | Modern Tell el-Mutesellim; large town in northern Israel controlling a large north-south road |
| *menit* | A broad necklace or beaded collar with symbolic meaning, also used as musical instrument, i.e. rattle |
| *Meriu* | Locality in the Levant |
| *Min* | Anthropomorphic ityphallic fertility god, known since |

| | |
|---|---|
| | prehistoric times; often associated with Amun |
| *Mnevis* | Sacred bull associated with the god Atum |
| *Monthu* | Falcon-headed war god |
| *Naharina* | Egyptian name for the empire of the Mitanni |
| *Neferbau-Semseru* | Minor deity |
| *Nefertem* | Youthful anthropomorphic primordial god wearing a lotus flower on the head, closely connected to the sun |
| *Negeba* | Negev desert |
| *Nephthys* | Anthropomorphic goddess of relatively late date, in mythology sister of Osiris and Isis |
| *Nepri* | Hermaphrodite personification of the grain |
| *Nine Bow peoples* | Term for the foreign peoples inhabiting the world, ideally ruled by the Egyptian king, the number 'nine' symbolising the plural of the plural ('three' in Egyptian terms) |
| *Nome* | Administrative district in Ancient Egypt |
| *Nut* | Anthropomorphic celestial goddess, wife of the earth god Geb, often depicted bent in a high arch over his body with stars on her body. Every night she swallows the sun before giving birth to it once more in the morning |
| *Nyi* | Apamea (modern Qal'at el Mudik) at the river Orontes |
| *Osiris* | Anthropomorphic chthonic fertility god depicted in mummy form with green skin, mainly known in his aspect as ruler of the underworld; in mythology murdered and dismembered by his brother Seth, then reassembled and properly buried by his wife and sister Isis |
| *Pekhuu-netj* | Unidentified region |
| *Peret season* | One of the three seasons in the Egyptian year, associated with emergence of the crops, equivalent to spring |
| *Peten* | An area in the Delta near the Bitter Lakes |
| *Ptah* | Anthropomorphic mummy-form creator god and patron of craftsmen with main seat in Memphis; he creates through thought and speech |

| | |
|---|---|
| *Punt* | African land, probably located in modern Eritrea or Somalia; goal of Egyptian expeditions to trade for exotic goods such as myrrh and frankincense, exotic timbers and animals, etc |
| *Qat* | Unidentified region |
| *Qedut* | Unidentified locality |
| *Re* | Solar god, sometimes viewed as king of the gods, closely associated with kingship, often linked to other gods, e.g. Amun or Horakhty. During the day he travels with his retinue in a bark across the sky, at night he is swallowed by the sky goddess Nut and travels through the underworld until his rebirth in the morning |
| *Retjenu* | Part of ancient Canaan, roughly located in modern Lebanon |
| *Sekhmet* | 'The Mighty': lion-headed war goddess and bringer of illness and epidemics |
| *Sendjar* | Modern Sheizar in Asia Minor |
| *Seth* | Closely linked in early periods to Horus as a second aspect of kingship, later becoming his adversary; also in later mythology viewed as brother and murderer of Osiris; lord of the desert and the foreign lands; defends the solar bark during its night time travels across the underworld against the giant snake trying to stop its progress |
| *Seven Hathors* | Since the New Kingdom in popular belief a group of goddesses foretelling destiny |
| *Sharuhen* | Town in southern Palestine |
| *Shemu season* | One of the three Egyptian seasons equivalent to harvest time |
| *sistrum* | Musical instrument: a rattle with a handle in the form of the goddess Hathor |
| *Sobek* | Crocodile or crocodile-headed god embodying the fertility of the Nile water, mainly worshipped in places where many crocodiles lived, e.g. the Fayum |
| *Son of Re* | One of the five titles of the pharaoh; the latest in the sequence, going back to the fourth dynasty, thereafter frequently used |

| | |
|---|---|
| *Sopdu* | God of the eastern margin of the Delta, depicted either as a falcon idol or a Bedouin |
| *Ta-aa-na-ka* | Taanach; locality 8km south-east of Megiddo |
| *Thoth* | Ibis-headed lunar god and lord of knowledge, patron of scribes, also depicted as ibis or baboon |
| *Tikhesi* | A land near Kadesh on the river Orontes |
| *Tja-ru* | Locality in the Levant |
| *Two-Ladies* | One of the five titles of the pharaoh |
| *uraeus* | Greek version of an Egyptian word, 'the rearing one', referring to an attacking cobra, symbol of kingship. |
| *Walls of the Ruler* | String of fortresses along the eastern Delta |
| *Wawat* | Egyptian name for the area between the first and second Nile cataract, part of Nubia |
| *Ways of Horus* | Coastal route from the eastern Delta to the Levant |
| *Wennefer* | Epithet and special form of Osiris: 'the perfect being' |
| *Wentiu* | Inhabitants of the land Wenet (not located so far) |
| *Wepwawet* | 'Opener of the ways': canine god closely connected to the very early kings when his image was carried in front of the king on his campaigns |
| *Wereret* | Goddess of Punt: 'the great one' |
| *Yaa* | Probably an area in ancient Canaan |
| *Ye-khem* | Modern Khirbet Jimma in the Levant |